# What's Right with the Church?

# What's Right with the Church?

## G. AVERY LEE

**BROADMAN PRESS**
Nashville, Tennessee

**TO**

**three young churchmen**

**Jeni-Su**
**Gee**
**Greg**

# Preface

Constant listening and reading about what is wrong with the church led me to feel that something ought to be said in its favor. One expects criticism to come from outside the ranks of the church. And those who love it most dearly ought also to reprove it in love. There are weaknesses in the church, to be sure; but there is also much strength. A popular song of the 1940s went:

> You've got to accentuate the positive,
> Eliminate the negative,
> Latch on to the affirmative,
> Don't mess with Mr. In-Between.

Something like that needs to be said for the church.

I am not sociologist enough, nor ethicist-theologian enough to take a point by point apologetic to the likes of Martin R. Marty, Gibson Winter, Peter Berger, or Harvey Cox, to name but a few "friends" of the church. However, there is the feeling that in the week-by-week pastoral ministry there is offered ample opportunity to deal with the church and its members both critically and lovingly in a positive, constructive manner. Hence, this little offering on WHAT'S RIGHT WITH THE CHURCH?

The material has been used in one way or another with the church of which I am pastor. Also, it was used with the Wake Forest Baptist Church of Wake Forest, North Carolina. These are good churches. Not what they ought to be, of course; nevertheless, good churches composed of people who want to "be" the church, whatever that means. I am grateful to each congregation for their helpful, hopeful attitude.

I also express appreciation to my secretary, Mrs. John Hendrix, for typing the manuscript.

G. AVERY LEE
ST. CHARLES AVENUE BAPTIST CHURCH
NEW ORLEANS, LOUISIANA

# CONTENTS

I LOVE THY KINGDOM, LORD,
THE HOUSE OF THINE ABODE,
THE CHURCH OUR BLEST REDEEMER SAVED
WITH HIS OWN PRECIOUS BLOOD.

I LOVE THY CHURCH, O GOD!
HER WALLS BEFORE THEE STAND,
DEAR AS THE APPLE OF THINE EYE,
AND GRAVEN ON THY HAND.

FOR HER MY TEARS SHALL FALL;
FOR HER MY PRAY'RS ASCEND;
TO HER MY TOILS AND CARES BE GIV'N,
TILL TOILS AND CARES SHALL END.

BEYOND MY HIGHEST JOY
I PRIZE HER HEAV'NLY WAYS,
HER SWEET COMMUNION, SOLEMN VOWS,
HER HYMNS OF LOVE AND PRAISE.

SURE AS THY TRUTH SHALL LAST,
TO ZION SHALL BE GIV'N
THE BRIGHTEST GLORIES EARTH CAN YIELD,
AND BRIGHTER BLISS OF HEAV'N.

TIMOTHY DWIGHT

# I

# A Fellowship of Concerned Friends

## Matthew 16:18

If the church can survive its friends, it has little to fear from its enemies. The church has always been subjected to criticism from the outside. But in the past decade, and more especially in the past five years, voices inside the church have told of its *Suburban Captivity,* urged it to *Renewal,* spoken of the *Noise of* (its) *Solemn Assemblies,* and caused it to sit squirming in its *Comfortable Pews.*

There are voices of pessimism tolling the death knell, saying (some with seeming morbid delight), "The church is dead!" Or, if not quite so drastic, at least they claim that the church is sick unto death. Listen to one: "The church in the city is in panic, the church in the suburbs is sunk in complacency, and the church in town and country exhibits symptoms of rigor mortis." [1]

I have never been able to agree that ours is a post-Christian era or that the church is dead. The church does have its problems, to be sure. It is not as healthy as it should be. But I am a firm believer that God never leaves himself without a witness. Perhaps the church, as we know it, may fade away, but something will arise to take its place. Even Elijah learned that he was not the only one who had not bowed to Baal.

Novelist Monia Furlong has a book entitled *With Love to the Church*. I like that! Because of our own love affair with the church, we insiders want it to be its best. I have done my share of criticizing the church for its not being what it could or should be. In trying to get church members into a state of excited caring, I, too, have used such phrases as "cut-flower civilization." But I find myself more and more asking, From what rooted flowers have we been cut? Was it when our grandfathers sold rotten meat to the army or patent opiates to the sick before there were Pure Food and Drug laws? Or when worthless stock was sold to investors before there was some bit of protection from a Securities Exchange?

Ours has been labeled the "post-Christian era." But what era before ours was truly Christian? Was it the Crusades, the Spanish Inquisition, or the New England witch hunts?

Or we say that we are "living on borrowed capital." But not all of our forefathers gave us sound spiritual stock; some did. Not all their children are living on borrowed capital; some are. Some are making some heavy invest-ments in Christian living for tomorrow's generation.

No period of history could be classified as a Christian era with a Christian civilization with total Christian stock. The church has never been perfect. We could hope that someday it might, and we can work toward that end, realizing that the church is composed of imperfect human beings.

In the year 1816, John Keats said (about churches), "They are dying like an outburst lamp." But he forgot something. As another puts it: "The first essential of a quiet funeral is a willing corpse." That the church from Keats' time to ours has not been a willing corpse is evi-dent. The greatest expansion of the church has been in the first half of the twentieth century.

The most optimistic man I know concerning the future of the church and Christian faith is one of my former pro-fessors at Yale, Kenneth Scott Latourette—the world's foremost authority on the history and expansion of Chris-tianity.

I recently wrote this old professor-friend, asking if he still maintained his optimism concerning the church. In typical professorial manner, he answered by referring me to two of his more recent books: *Christianity Through the Ages*, and Volume V of his series, *Christianity in a Revolutionary Age*. Yes, he is still optimistic, with much evidence in his favor. Listen to him:

As a religion Christianity has had a wider geographic spread and is more deeply rooted among more people than any other religion in the history of mankind.[2]

The age may seem evil and the close be either at hand or far off, but we Christians must continue to witness, seeking to bring all men to discipleship and to lead them to obedience to what Jesus taught his disciples.[3]

## What Is the Church?

At the outset let us consider what the church is. The New Testament teaches that the church is made up of those who in repentant faith accept Jesus Christ as Lord. Out of this teaching have grown two concepts: (1) the church is a local congregation of believers; (2) the church is the total body of believers in Christ, known as "the body of Christ." A Christian is a part of both groups.

A decade ago, Elton Trueblood coined a phrase which captured the attention of many church folk. He described the church as "the fellowship of the concerned." By that he meant concern about the fact of sin, the need of a Saviour, the need of society for a group of believers to pattern themselves after Christ as a demonstration of what true Christianity really is.

More recently, Trueblood used another descriptive phrase, "the company of the committed," as the title of a book. In it he says that despite the popularity of churchgoing, "There are millions of back-pew Christians" causing high attendance at church and low Christian influence in the world. A task force of committed Christians could revitalize the church and revolutionize society, he declares. We could say that no one can really be a Christian without committing himself to the will of God, for Christianity involves *doing* as well as *believing*.

Of course, we know the church has weaknesses. After all, it is composed of human beings who themselves are weak. Those of us who are constituents of the church do not measure up to either its teachings or demands. For that matter, what member of any organization—Rotary, Kiwanis, Masons, Daughters of the American Revolution, Fraternity, and the like—fully live up to even the human ideals of their group? Yet, who is concerned with their weakness or who points out their foibles, other than an occasional Sinclair Lewis?

Those who are most actively participating in the church are the first to admit that judgment must begin in the house of God, among the members of the household of faith. We who love the church are the ones most concerned about correcting its faults and strengthening its weaknesses, yet we are the ones who most consistently speak of its faults.

Does a real estate agent tell us the unfavorable features of the property he is trying to sell? "Well, the neighborhood isn't so good anymore. The contractor who built the house was not exactly honest and reliable, but . . ."

Can you imagine a car salesman talking down his automobile to a prospective buyer? "We've had nothing but trouble with this model. It drinks gasoline, has no power, and is our service shop's best friend."

Would an insurance broker point out the weaknesses of his company as he tries to sell a policy? "This is a new company, and it is just now building its reserves. Why, if we had five hundred claims all at once, we would be bankrupt!"

No, you never hear salesmen talk that way. Sometimes

we wish they *would* be more honest in their representations.

In a manner of speaking, Christians are salesmen on the highest plane. We do need to reevaluate the church so as to know our product better. Whatever its defects, they must be corrected—*from the inside.* Just as manufacturers strive constantly for better products, so must the church. As salesmen are trained to emphasize the best features, so must church members be able to point out the positive aspects of the church . . . and be committed to its truth.

In asking for commitment to the church, we assume that it is worthy of our devotion. If the church is of God, then believers in Jesus Christ should consign themselves wholeheartedly to it. In an open, dedicated commitment of ourselves to what is right with the church we can go out into an openly hostile world to present the claims of Christ and the necessity of the church. Therefore, in asking for such dedication, we must answer the question, *what is right with the church?*

One thing that is right with the church is its foundation. We sing, "The church's one foundation is Jesus Christ her Lord," and we are right. Christ founded the church and is himself its foundation. Following Peter's confession of Christ as Son of the living God, Jesus said, "On this rock I will build my church"—not on the man, Peter, but upon Peter's confession of faith. And Ephesians 2:19–20 reminds us: "You are fellow citizens with the saints and members of the household of God, built upon the foundation of the apostles and prophets, Christ Jesus himself being the chief cornerstone" (RSV).

It is always dangerous to put an organization around an idea if you want the idea to live. Yet, ideas must have some structure, despite the danger. Old time Judaism, the religion of the Jews, had tremendous spiritual power, but it had degenerated into an organization that was more intent on keeping itself alive than it was on enlivening the environment with its power. It had become politically corrupt and was more concerned with the letter of the law than its spiritual purpose. Given to splitting hairs on moral issues, it released little of its inherent moral and spiritual power. Unfortunately, this has happened time and again in Christian history, and is happening in today's church, more concerned with itself as an institution than with its spiritual vitality.

For example, an endowed church runs the great risk of becoming complacent. One church had a bequest which left them wealthy. Stock was sold to pay off their total indebtedness, and they still had $1,250,000! Official meetings are now more concerned with the business of the fluctuating stock market than with what Jesus called "the Father's business."

No doubt, Jesus desired the church to be a spiritual force, in a real sense. He also knew there is such a thing as spirit without body and body without spirit. The spirit is more important than the body. The spirit may remain strong after the body is old and weak. It even survives after the body is dead. But in the world the spirit and the body go together. The spirit wears the body, and the body is infused with the spirit.

The spirit of the church is more important than its body —that is, its building, its organization, or its denomination.

The body is the institution known as the church. Jesus could not see a purely spiritual religion, for Christianity must take form in a company of dedicated, committed believers. It was this way from the first. It was this way at Pentecost. It must always be this way, for Christianity cannot be separated from people.

### Concerned Believers

A second thing that is right with the church, a natural outgrowth of being founded on Christ, is that the church is a family of concerned believers.

The symbol of becoming a Christian is birth, the "new birth," for it begins an entirely new kind of life. The new birth is like the physical birth in that there is conception, gestation, actual birth, and growth into maturity. In the physical life we are born, not only into life, but also into a family. The family is an organic unit and it exists, among other things, to produce more births, more new lives. It has to for its very survival. But the family relationship of living, loving, and growing together is important, too.

The church is Christ's family. The essence of Christianity is this family relationship. God is the Heavenly Father, Christ is the Elder Brother, and we follow as his children in our spiritual home, the church.

There are some erroneous ideas about Christianity. Some think that being a Christian is merely following the Golden Rule or the Sermon on the Mount. That is all very well, but it is not starting at the right place. A child is first born into the family physically or through legal adoption. Then he grows into the family pattern, carries the family heritage, and assumes family responsibility.

Similarly, one is born spiritually into the family of God; he grows, develops, matures in identity, and shows forth the Christian family. Anyone who thinks he can just dip into the New Testament and pick out a piece of morality, then go off and live it on his own has another think coming. He had better exercise his option and think again, for he has missed the fundamental idea of what Christianity is all about.

If one way of entering the Christian family is via "the new birth," this lays upon those already within the family the necessity of presenting the claims of Christ to those who are not Christian. This is called evangelism.

## Evangelism

There are numerous "plans of evangelism" and multiple gimmicks used to manipulate people. However, nothing can replace one believing Christian sharing his faith with an unbeliever.

In a recent meeting of pastors of a city ministerial association, the chairman of the evangelism committee excitedly presented what he said was the most thrilling new approach to evangelism he had seen in years. Pioneered, he said, by the Missouri Lutherans, it offered unlimited possibilities because it involved the person-to-person approach. The Baptists in the group could hardly believe their ears when the man described "the marked New Testament" approach. We have been teaching that in seminary evangelism classes for years. But to these men it was an exciting new idea.

Before hooting at them, we had better see how faithful we have been in the task of personal evangelism. If we are tired of an old method, let us find some new approach to the same responsibility.

An active sports program can be an effective evangelistic agency of a church, especially among youth. It can work with adults, too. Take one church and its Royal Ambassador basketball program, for example.

This church has a very active Royal Ambassador program which includes more than sports, but it began with this emphasis. In a four-year period, it has grown from nothing to perhaps fifty boys in the three age classifications—Crusaders, Pioneers, and Ambassadors. A trophy case is filling up with awards won by these boys. More important, there are spiritual trophies, too.

The first year, three boys came to play basketball. One was a Roman Catholic, one had no church affiliation, and the third came with a reform school record. The Catholic boy remains Catholic, but he has gained a good knowledge of the Scriptures, Baptist doctrine, and an appreciation for Baptists. Because of distance, one began regular attendance at a Baptist mission. The third made a profession of faith, was baptized, and remains an active member of the church. Next year he goes to a church-related college on an academic-music scholarship.

A Jewish lad secured permission from his rabbi and his parents to join the Royal Ambassadors in order to play basketball. His parents and his rabbi were told that he would be required to learn Christian doctrine, which would include learning what Christians call "the plan of salvation," as well as many New Testament Scripture verses. Nevertheless, they agreed.

At one game there was an amusing incident. Each game

begins with the Royal Ambassador motto, "Go forward in Christ's name." This Jewish boy said to the pastor, "About that motto, could I say, 'Go forward in Moses' name?'" The boy remains a Jew at this point, but there is an avenue of approach that was not open before.

Right now, there are several boys in the program who have no church relationship, nor do their parents. In addition, there are others who belong to churches but have lack of biblical and Christian knowledge. They may not become Baptists, but they will become more enlightened Christians.

A third rightness about the church is that its avowed purpose is to bring all of life under its sway.

When Jesus founded the church, he gave it a task: "Go into all the world and make disciples . . . for you are my witnesses . . . teach them to observe what I have taught you to observe."

Christianity must be a growing movement that captures the lives and loyalties of more and more persons, communities, and nations.

Some twenty years back, the American Baptist Convention had a program which I liked very much. The slogans they used were an excellent outline of the task of the church:

Reach all you can for Christ.

Win all you reach.

Teach all you win.

Train all you teach.

Enlist all you train.

The process starts all over again as the enlisted ones win others.

If any institution is to bring life under its sway it must be a living organism. Biologists say that a living organism has four functions: sensitivity, movement, assimilation, and reproduction. Let us take a brief look at these functions as they might relate to the church.

First, *sensitivity*—a feeling for that which lies around. Is the church sensitive to the condition of the world? Is it receiving impressions from those in its own neighborhood? Does the church know the feeling of oppression, economic injustice, discrimination because of skin color, social barriers erected according to whether a man works with his hands or his brain? Even more, is the church concerned about the some seventy-six million people who claim no affiliation with church or synagogue?

Second, *movement*—the church has made progressive movement, even if it has been terribly slow and sometimes horribly late. But movement must continue in its forward effort for the church to remain alive. We know full well that when forward movement stops, there is a momentary pause, then a backward movement sets in.

Third, *assimilation*—the act or process of bringing into likeness or resemblance or identity. That is, the church must bring the secular world into a likeness of itself. Therein lies the pattern of the future: to bring the world into a resemblance of Jesus Christ. And the tragic thing is that so many have done so little.

Finally, *reproduction*—not to be confused with assimilation, to bring into likeness. Reproduction is to bring new life. It is a part of the creative process. In the church this reproductive process takes place in two ways. In his conversation with Nicodemus, Jesus said that a person must be born again. Thus individuals, already physically alive, must be born spiritually. Then, as Paul puts it, Christ must not only be born in us, but must relive in us.

Following these functions of a living organism, the church can bring all life under its sway.

### Personal Need for the Church

The church is right and essential because *we personally need it*.

Many times a person will start off on an individualistic approach to Christian faith only to discover that he cannot go it alone. We need the inspiration of others who are going along the same route. We need their encouragement and fellowship. Others help us and we help them. The interplay of Christian love and service within the family of Christ trains us for love and service toward those who are outside the family.

We must be continually reminded of the fellowship within the church. We may not like all the people in the church, but we are *brothers*, members of the same family. We may not approve all the conduct of our fellow members, but the church—on its human side—is not a showplace. While the conduct of its members does reflect on the church, either to its credit or distraction, it is not necessarily a place where people are put on exhibition.

On its divine side, the church is a source of spiritual power. It is a place where we go to replenish and refill our empty, barren lives. And, unfortunately, some of us have shallow vessels in which to hold this treasure.

On its human side, the church is a school where people learn. It is a hospital where sick souls find health. It is

a place where people are learning how to live. The people
of the church have not "arrived," they are merely on the
road, traveling, headed toward Zion, with their faces
thitherward.

There has been considerable interest in lay theological
studies, with revived concern as to the proper, valid place
of service on the part of the laity. With our Baptist emphasis on "the priesthood of the believer" and on an in-
formed membership, we need to be conscious of and to use
this current concern. To be sure, there has been effort in
the Training Union, Brotherhood, and in the study course
approach. The new Life and Work Curriculum will be
an added improvement. But all these are inadequate fully
to reach into these modern desires, for such groups as
Laity Lodge in Texas and Elton Trueblood's Yokefellows
are flourishing.

One church has used Findley Edge's book *A Quest for
Vitality in Religion* for such a layman's study group. The
book was divided into three sections. A resource person
gave an introduction to each section, and three laymen
spoke briefly at pertinent points. Then there was discussion leading to involvement.

I. How Can a Baptist Church Fulfil Its Purpose?
   A. The church's ministry as I understand it
   B. What is obsolete about today's churches
   C. How I see our church in this community
II. The Nature of Man and His Need for Christian Fel-
    lowship
   A. Man's relationship to God as I understand it
   B. An approach to everyday spiritual living

C. What I think the church can do to help laymen understand their spiritual natures

III. The Real Meaning of Faith and an Approach to Evangelism
   A. How I discovered the meaning of faith
   B. Why I think laymen lose interest in Christian witnessing
   C. How to get laymen interested in evangelism

## Victory over Evil

There is one other thing. The church is right because we cannot hope to have victory over the forces of evil in this world if we try to fight the battle alone.

The Bible pictures the encounter of good with evil as light against darkness. Someone has said, "I'd rather light a candle than sit and curse the darkness." Well, one little candle *does* overpower the darkness in its small area. One or two or even a hundred will not do it, but put eighty-thousand candles in the New Orleans Sugar Bowl Stadium and the sky will light up for miles around. So it is in the battle against evil. One Christian shows evil for what it is, but a concentrated group of Christians can put evil to flight.

The old, eternal power of evil is always with us. But in the past generation this power has created for itself an engine of destruction the like of which our world has seldom seen. Let none of us ever underestimate the power and force of evil. Evil is organized, and efficiently so. It is dedicated to the task of stamping out everything that is right and good. Evil's major objective is to eliminate the church. Any attack on the church is considered legitimate.

So, discord, discontent, unfounded accusations, the casting of aspersions, and the stirring up of suspicion is valid in attacking the church.

No individual religious expression can cope with evil's colossal power. When people talk about having "their own kind of religion," you may be sure that they are apart from the stream of the historic church. They are often sentimental, and more often complacent. They have seldom, if ever, contemplated the real task of Christianity on earth: the deliverance of men from the clutches of sin.

Do you think that an individualistic religion can hope to stand up against the forces of evil that are let loose in today's world? If so, you are doing some unrealistic thinking. All of us—believers in God, believers in Christ, believers in man and in freedom—all churches, all Christians must stand side by side, for nothing else will do.

To be sure, I believe that the righteousness of God will ultimately prevail whether you or I have a part in it or not. If we fail, God will use some other means, some other people; for God cannot be defeated. But the church is a visible expression of God at work. And, I believe there are expressions of God at work outside the church, too.

After reading this list of things that I consider to be right about the church, you might think this to be a surface sort of analysis. And you may be right. But I hope that as we go along, that which is considered surface may be seen in more depth. You might well ask: What has all this to do with us? Most of us are believers, we are members of the church . . . some church.

That is probably true. But the degree and the quality of our churchmanship, our commitment, is another matter.

Let me discuss this in terms of emphasis which my two immediate predecessors in my present pastorate stressed. During his pastorate, Dr. J. Lyn Elder stressed the word *community*, togetherness. That was a vitally needed element at the time, for there was much separateness in the congregation. Then came Dr. Myron C. Madden, who underscored *koinōnia*, the welding together of a variety of factors into a marvelous "fellowship of difference." My own accent has been upon *commitment*, a dedication that would share this fellowship with others. I believe this is a true meaning of the doctrine of the priesthood of the believer. It is a natural outgrowth of our faith in Jesus Christ as Lord.

Some readers may not be professing believers in Christ. You say you know you ought to be, that you want to, and that you plan to. All right, now is the opportunity for you to do something about it. Publicly acknowledge Jesus Christ as your Saviour. Openly commit yourself to Christ and the church. Otherwise, your staying out only adds to the forces arrayed against it.

Among Southern Baptists it is said that there are some three million persons who are unaffiliated with a church in the community where they live. Are you one of them? Have you ever considered what kind of a testimony your lack of affiliation, your lack of identification, your lack of commitment is giving to others? Your staying outside may well be interpreted as saying that you do not consider the church worthwhile.

More than anything, Christians want other people to be identified with Christ and his church. They want others to become a part of the fellowship of the concerned, the company of the committed. This means some changes.

For some, it means a complete change of life—away from sin, through the new birth, into the family of God.

For some Baptists, it means a change of church home.

For yet others, it may mean a completely new alignment with a new group of fellow Christians.

If you believe in Christ as your Saviour and if you believe in the church—that the church's one foundation is Jesus Christ, that the church is the family of believers, that the purpose of the church is to bring all of life under the influence of Christ, that the church is essential in the struggle against all forms of evil, that you personally need the church—then, you are invited to become a part of the fellowship of the committed so that you can begin showing your friendship for the church and your commitment to its rightness.

## Notes

1. Shirley Greene, "Some Clouds on a Summer Day," *The Christian Century*, July 1, 1964, p. 854.

2. Kenneth Scott Latourette, *Christianity Through the Ages* (New York: Harper & Row, 1965), p. ix.

3. *Ibid.*, p. 309.

# 2

# A Fellowship of Sinners

## Mark 12:13–17

Of all the startling facts about the church, perhaps the most amazing is that it openly advertises itself as a "fellowship of sinners"—sinners saved by the grace of God, to be sure, but sinners. Try to get into any group by confessing your sin and see how far you get. Some groups will keep you out if they feel you have done something of which they disapprove. Other organizations will kick you out if they learn of some misdemeanor. Even the church has been guilty at this point.

In earlier days some of the "church fathers" were so insistent upon what they called discipline that they bear a heavy burden of guilt for lives they caused to be lost in effective service to Christ and the church. If a lad or lass went to a dance, for example, he or she might be brought before the church in scorn. Charges would be preferred and fellowship withdrawn. A man who is now an outstanding bishop of a Methodist church in the South was "kicked out" of a Baptist church because in his youth he attended a dance. On the other hand, one of the most valuable Baptist church members I have ever pastored was removed from a Methodist church because she did the same thing.

Fortunately, these two were not lost to service. But far too often those "removed ones" have remained cut off, adrift, lost to usefulness in the church because some church members forgot that they, too, are sinners.

Dr. Charles Laurence was a regular attendant at both Sunday School and church. Yet, he was an unaffiliated Baptist for some sixty-five years! He had been removed from a church roll because as a youth he went to a barn dance! I am not excusing him for his stubbornness in refusing to reunite with a church that did want him. But neither can I absolve those who were responsible for withdrawing their fellowship from him. Yes, we may have lost something in our drifting away from church discipline. But we must never forget that each church member is a sinner, too.

### Sinners All

In the second century, Celsus, the pagan philosopher, jeered at the Christians because they referred to themselves as sinners. To the pagan world it seemed a ridiculous thing that a group of people should openly advertise themselves as sinners. And not only that, but they actually invited other known sinners to come in and associate with them. Why, everyone knows the social axiom that "a person is known by the company he keeps." Even Jesus did not escape the smear technique known currently as "guilt by association," for it was said of Jesus: "This man receives sinners, and eats with them" (Luke 15:2, RSV).

There are today, unfortunately, church members *and churches* who try to avoid all association with sinners. How many churches, for example, just at the time when the needs around them are greatest, pack up and move to a new location where "our kind of people" live? In such fashion we do get away from some of the ugliness of sin, and from some of the cries and burdens of sin and human misery. But that may be a terribly high price to pay. We may also be getting ourselves away from him who came to save sinners.

You see, whenever a church gets so respectable that it no longer welcomes sinners, at that point it ceases to be the church—*and,* more important, it ceases to be Christian!

In Mark's account of the calling of Levi (Matthew), there is a sentence which draws attention to a secret we seem to have forgotten. Mark says, "Many tax collectors and sinners were sitting down with Jesus." Jesus knew how to appeal to and draw the irreligious, the sinners.

This dinner party which Mark describes is far removed from the common run of our church affairs, whether it be the time of worship or the social occasion. The modern counterparts of the tax collectors and sinners do not sit in great numbers with today's church folk. In the average

Sunday congregation, if there are as many as half a dozen unrepentant sinners, it is unusual. At most social affairs of the church this is likewise true. Even when church members are given definite assignments to bring a "tax collector," they often dillydally around and forget to extend the invitation until too late.

It is uncomfortably disturbing to think that the very people for whom Jesus had the greatest appeal are conspicuously absent from our church world. We may be correct in saying, "It's their own fault. They know the church is here." But is that all we can say? Is that making our escape from reality too easy? We do have a responsibility for getting these people with us, you know.

Sometimes we rejoice greatly over the church membership of a college president, an outstanding athlete, the chairman of a corporation board, an unusual professional man, or a prominent citizen. We usually put forth a lot of effort to enlist such people in church. They are often featured as special speakers on programs. But what about some of the "lesser children of the earth?" Do we exult as much when one of them comes into the church? Do we put forth as much effort to reach them? Jesus did! After all, there is great rejoicing in heaven when any sinner repents.

It is easy enough to be in charge of the devotional service at the city jail or the rescue mission. But what about more demanding service? How do we receive that kind of sinner if he makes a profession of faith or even desires to move his membership to our church while still in jail?

One group of Christians is responsible for literacy classes in the county prison, teaching inmates to read and write. They go beyond the teaching into active efforts of rehabilitation and job opportunity after release. They try to lead the persons into active community life and participation in the church. They also guide the church into an acceptance of these "sinners" as a part of the church fellowship.

Joe Marlowe was such a person. He had been in the best and worst of jails from coast to coast. A Baptist deacon who was in charge of a Gideon service at the county road camp deserves much credit. Repeated visits, talks, prayer, and a personal reading of a marked New Testament led to Joe's conversion. The camp supervisor accompanied him to church for his baptism. A job was waiting for him at his release. The church and the community accepted him as he was—"a sinner saved by grace." He was received with rejoicing into the church fellowship and became a staunch supporter.

In the Scott County jail in Georgetown, Kentucky, a Mrs. Effie Cochran was being held on an alleged murder charge for killing her husband. Mrs. J. W. Faust, a worker with the Kentucky Welfare Association and a member of the Georgetown Baptist Church, went to talk with the woman. She stopped at the jail and found Mrs. Cochran convicted of her sin and ready to accept Christ as Saviour. The county judge, Charles Brooking, a Baptist deacon, arranged for Mrs. Cochran to attend the Georgetown church without police escort.

When the invitation was given, Mrs. Cochran made her public profession of faith in Christ, asked for baptism and membership in the church, was unanimously received, and was baptized at the evening service. She returned to jail following her baptism. Later, other members of the church put up her bond and took her into their home to live until her trial.

Following her conversion, jailer George Wise said, "Mrs. Cochran is an excellent prisoner. She helps my wife a great deal around the jail and is really sincere in this newfound Christian life." And Mrs. Faust said, "I never felt better in my life. A person can never realize what this has meant to me."

Pastor Dan Moore, reporting the incident, said that this was "the story of three people whose personal witness made news." Besides Mrs. Faust and Mrs. Cochran, "The third witness was that of newspaperman Billy Thompson (a member of the Georgetown church and sportswriter for the Lexington Herald). . . . He was present when Mrs. Cochran made her profession of faith and felt that he too could be a witness by putting the story into print."[1] And he did.

### The Nature of the Church

An ancient phrase has come to be used as a general expression to describe the church: *the communion of saints.*

This concept of the church assumes that the church is composed of good people who are fairly confident of their own standing in the sight of God.

The comment of the outsider who looks at actual churches composed of persons who are all-too-obviously human, sometimes quarreling among themselves, often prosaic and joyless, generally conventional and timid where they ought to be revolutionary and bold, would be: "So! this is the communion of saints! Well, show me how they are any better, any different, any more saintly than I am."

To be sure, there are many who do feel this way: who feel that they are as just, honest, generous, and kind as any church members, and feel that being inside a church fellowship would make them no better. And they may be right—they may not be any better. But *to be better* is not the point of the church.

Such an attitude indicates a total misunderstanding of the nature of the church. The attitude is a kind of claim that no true Christian ever dares to make for himself. A Christian never dares to think he can live at his best in his own strength without God's help, without a knowledge of God's Word, reinforced by faith and prayer, and renewed and supported by the fellowship of the church.

Insofar as the church is "the communion of saints," it is always by God's designation and never by man's self-appointment. The true saints are always taken by surprise in being so designated, as were the righteous in Jesus' parable: "Lord, when saw we thee hungred and fed thee?" (Matt. 25:37). The real saints are those who, without any suspicion of saintliness, minister "unto the least of these" and then discover, to their utter amazement, that Christ accepts these acts of love and kindness as being done unto him.

From the standpoint of its membership and its message, the church is more accurately described as *the communion of sinners*.

Using this descriptive phrase, let us take a look at the church as a fellowship of sinners.

For one thing, the church is not composed of persons

who have any claim to superior goodness, although some church members may act that way. The church is made up of people who know better than anyone else that *they are not good*. The Christian is not the moral man, nor the just man, nor the socially responsible man. His life may take on all these qualities, as indeed it should. But the qualities are derivative of something else. The Christian is, first of all, a forgiven man, a redeemed person. He knows the utter realism of his wrongness, but he has found the assurance that even in the midst of his evil, he is loved and forgiven.

But, for one reason or another, people inside and outside the church find this difficult to grasp and even more difficult to accept, either for themselves or for others. Perhaps there are two reasons for this.

The outstanding Jewish New Testament scholar, C. G. Montefiore, in his book *The Synoptic Gospels*, points out that the rabbis would not have criticized Jesus merely because he cared for the poor, the outcast, the sinner. They, too, would have welcomed the repentant sinner. What is new and radically different is that Jesus actually *sought out* the sinner. Montefiore indicates that if we deny Jesus' originality in this connection, or negate his opening of new avenues in men's attitudes toward sin and sinners we would be doing the same as beating our heads against the wall.

So, one reason for criticizing Jesus would be that he not only welcomed sinners but sought them out; he deliberately tried to bring them into his fellowship. The sinner finds it hard to believe that anyone wants him. And the insider, who himself has been wanted, sought out, and found, questions whether or not the sinner actually ought to be sought out.

Second, the Pharisees objected to Jesus' acts rather than his words. This is really nothing more than a restatement of what I have been saying. It was the act of eating with sinners that bothered them. They could stand a lot of verbal teaching. They did a lot of that themselves. What bothered them was the action which made effective Jesus' words of invitation and acceptance. But Jesus always acted on what he said. Never was it what Jesus said that got him into trouble; it was what he did.

### Brotherhood

There is a parallel in our own time. No one objects to sending missionaries to Africa or to preaching to the Negro and trying to bring him to salvation. But, actually bringing him into the fellowship of one's own church, that's something else! Tell the Negro that God loves him and that Christ died for him; that's all right. But, to sit down at the table and eat with him, even at church at the Lord's table; that's another matter. Words are one thing, actions are another.

It is nearly always true that actions, not words, bring trouble. But actions must demonstrate the Christian message. Whenever a Christian acts on his faith, he is usually in for some kind of trouble. As often as not the trouble comes from within the fellowship of the church. It is not Christian teaching but Christian action that causes trouble. So, when one person or one church acts Christian, the sinner finds it hard to believe that he is wanted or included.

Perhaps the most vexing issue facing Southern churches
is that of race relations with the Negro. As more and more
civil rights are gained for the Negro by legislation, the
greater the need for responsible citizenship. Then, what
to do about the matter of interracial worship and church
membership? There is no easy solution.

One prominent Negro pastor said to his white counterpart: "Don't you think that I'm going to tell my people
to go over and join your church! I need every member I
can get, just as you do. And the ones that would join you,
I need most."

Another Negro pastor said to a group of white pastors:
"If I do not preach in favor of civil rights, I get in as much
trouble with my people as you do with yours if you do.
I understand your problems. Let us both be as Christian
as possible, for therein is our answer."

A good many Baptist churches have integrated their
membership with Negroes, usually without incident. Most
of these are in the border states, but a few are in the deep
South. Several Baptist associations and a few state conventions have Negro churches as members. North Carolina had
a joint session of the white and Negro state conventions
in 1965. The 1966 North Carolina Evangelistic Conference was a joint adventure, fully integrated with program
personnel and general attendance. New Orleans Baptists
are planning a city-wide, simultaneous revival involving
both white and Negro churches.

At the local church level, each congregation must, of
course, make its own decision. One church, facing all the
problems, listening to all the fears, finally voted on a
completely open membership. Some six months later, not

only did they have no Negro members, but they had not even had a Negro visitor. Despite the fact of wide publicity.

Another church, newly organized, fully integrated from the beginning, finds its stiffest competition from the old, established Negro church in the same community.

Some churches take the first step by accepting African students who are products of Baptist mission schools. This is a bit easier than taking the local Negro. Others go at the problem slowly, prayerfully, with serious discussion of as many implications as they can consider and begin a process of educating and leading the total membership to accept all worshipers and all as members who in repentant faith accept Jesus Christ as Saviour.

A new bank was opening in a large city. The president, not a Baptist, decided that a part of his Christian responsibility was to hire all new employees on the basis of their qualifications. One applicant was a Negro woman with several years' experience as a teller in the San Francisco Bank of America. She was well qualified, so she was hired; and on opening day, there she was. No one said a word, and that bank set an all-time record for opening day deposits in the United States.

If businessmen can set such an example—employing people on the basis of qualification—surely the church can practice what it preaches about there being no distinction in Christ.

### Sinners Forgiven

If we were to ask those who have given the most convincing testimonies about the meaning of the Christian

faith—if we could ask them what is the distinctive and
revolutionary element in their faith, that which makes all
the difference—each would probably give the same reply.
Paul, Augustine, Francis of Assissi, Martin Luther, John
Bunyan, John Wesley, Harry Emerson Fosdick, and Billy
Graham would probably agree that in the life, teaching,
ministry, death, and resurrection of Jesus Christ, we find
the forgiveness of sin that means restoration of fellowship
with God.

This is far more than philosophic idea or theological
doctrine. This is personal encounter, personal experience.
These men from different centuries, from different ecclesiastical backgrounds, found not only a belief in God's forgiveness of sin, but also the assurance that they had been
forgiven. *And so may we!*

Here, then, is the reason for the phrase "the fellowship
of sinners." We members of the church are alike in that,
first, we are all sinners; and second, we are sinners forgiven
by the grace of God. At this point, there is no such thing
as one church member's sin being less obnoxious, less serious than that of another, and that therefore, that member
is not so great a sinner as the other. Let one of us think
thus and it reveals that the sin of self-righteousness—self-
appointed sainthood—is still with us.

No, if sin separates from God, then it is any sin and it
is all sin which separates. Do you recall what Jesus said
in Luke 13:2–5?

"Do you think that these Galileans were worse sinners
than all the other Galileans, because they suffered thus?
. . . Or those . . . upon whom the tower in Siloam fell
and killed them, do you think that they were worse offend-

ers than all the others who dwelt in Jerusalem? I tell you, No; but unless you repent you will all likewise perish" (RSV).

Whenever a person sins, he is separated from God. Whenever he repents, he is forgiven, thus restored to fellowship with God. And he knows that all others in the fellowship of the redeemed are forgiven sinners, just as he is.

To be sure, the doctrine of forgiveness and the teaching of fellowship are not simple matters. They represent some of the supreme issues of our existence. For example, the entire matter of our personal freedom is involved. How shall we deal with the evil in life without at the same time reducing life to a subpersonal level where it is without choice, freedom, and responsibility? Almost everyone can see the necessity of something on the surface that looks like forgiveness. We cannot allow resentments and enmities to go on accumulating indefinitely. Vengeful animosity has to stop if we are not to exterminate one another.

But what do we do? Well, we say something like this: "Let's forgive and forget." Then we use a characteristically modern line of reasoning and say: "After all, he probably couldn't help it anyhow. His action was the result of bad environment, or early conditioning, or some traumatic experience of childhood. Knowing this, I can excuse him. To know all is to forgive all."

My soul, what a sense of self-righteousness that gives us! That is the kind of forgiveness that strips a person of all selfhood. We would leave that sinner as nothing more than a helpless pawn of resultant forces acting upon him in his environment. That is crass materialism! That denies the sacredness of human personality. Of course, circumstances and environment play a part, but they are not the whole matter: not in the Christian faith, and not in Christianity's teaching about man's personal, moral responsibility.

Christianity's teaching about forgiveness is the kind where the sinner is forgiven and at the same time *he is held accountable*. In the act of forgiveness God says (and so must we), "I forgive you. I believe you could have acted in a different manner; you could have done otherwise. Now, here is a new power to help you act differently from now on."

Only in that kind of forgiveness—with the assumption that you and I are persons with freedom of choice and moral responsibility—can we move toward the kind of restored personal fellowship with God that forgiveness of sin makes possible.

It is this fact that makes Christianity the *gospel*, that is, "the good news." Christianity does not tell us that we ought to be good, dupe us with trivial answers to our human problems, nor leave us with an easy optimism.

The gospel is no mere wistful thought that life is filled with possibilities for good, no mere fancy that goodwill is better than hatred, or that the world would be a nice place if we would only try harder to be loving, kind, and good.

We know that life includes the possibility of enormous evil, and this possibility is too often reality; that goodness is constantly being crushed to earth; and that we do not follow the ways of kindness and love.

There is loose among us what is thought to be a very broad, tolerant, up-to-date view of these matters. It can be expressed something like this: "I believe religion is a matter of being kind to one's fellows, being good to one's family, treating one's neighbor right, living by the Golden Rule, and being a good citizen. That's my religion."

That is all well and good. A person ought to do all those things. He is a sorry scoundrel if he does not. But to the person who says that that is his religion, I want to ask: "What does your religion do about you when you are not kind to your fellows, when you are not good to your family, when you do not treat your neighbor right, when you do not live by the Golden Rule, and when instead of being a good citizen, you are a downright rascal? What does your religion say to you then? What does it offer you?"

The good news of the Christian faith tells us that in Jesus Christ, God has stepped into the darkness of sin and evil. In our struggle with the flesh and the devil, with principalities and powers, with the real facts of life (self-deception, pride, immorality, meaninglessness, despair, anxiety, frustration, and fear), the Christian faith tells us that Jesus Christ has come into this warfare, too, and has conquered! Christ has conquered, not by condoning our sin and failure, but by refusing to disown us because of that failure and sin. He has conquered by holding us free and responsible, yet he forgives us and offers us another chance.

Some among us find that almost too good to be true. Because we may feel unloved, unwanted, and insecure among our fellows, we find it hard to believe that God loves us. But let that truth once break in upon us and we are never the same.

So! the church is not the community of the righteous, nor is it the communion of the saints. The church is a community of sinners, a fellowship of the redeemed—a fellowship of sinners forgiven by the grace of God and the love of Jesus Christ. The church openly proclaims itself as such, and pleads for other sinners to accept the same forgiveness and become a part of the company of the committed.

### Notes

1. *Western Recorder,* February 24, 1966.

# 3

## A Fellowship of the Suffering

### Galatians 6:2,5; 2 Corinthians 4:7—10,16—18

On a balmy night in June, 1965, I walked into the University Hospital in Madison, Wisconsin, where my wife, Ann, had been a patient for eight days and was to remain for six and a half more weeks. We talked of what she had been going through in the experience of pain and anxiety.

The next morning, I began to meet her fellow patients on Infirmary Third. It was an old section of the hospital, but what it lacked in modern facilities was far overshadowed by a tender, concerned care from excellent nurses and good orderlies. There I met Lauretta, Ann's room-

mate, afflicted with a horribly crippling arthritis. Her husband had brought her in and then had to return to their
Wisconsin farm. An elementary schoolteacher, she expressed her attitude in the words of a staunch Lutheran
faith: "Were it not for my faith in God, I couldn't go on."

And there was Gaynell, a lovely, young Negro woman
who had been the subject of a feature article in *Ebony*
magazine. She had a rare kind of disease, a tightening of
the skin—a horrible experience of torment. Of Gaynell,
her doctor said, "Every hospital should have her at least
once a month for what she does for patient morale." And
Gaynell told Ann, "Honey, when you just can't take no
more, ask the Lord for strength. He will give it to you."

And there was Jean, a young woman in her thirties,
diagnosed an epileptic . . . a college student having
rhino plastic surgery . . . a diabetic. Among these women
was a shared fellowship of suffering.

These women were strangers to one another, but not for
long. Being from different areas, cultures, races, and religions meant little to them. They were meeting on the
common ground of disease, pain, and suffering which
brought them into quick fellowship in their mutual need.
Here was true *koinōnia*. They began to bear one another's
burdens, to understand one another. They were walking a
lonely road, yet they were not alone. They had one another, and all of them had God walking with them, too.
Most of them acknowledged God's presence and were
ministering to one another out of their Christian faith.

Furthermore, they shared a human determination, a confidence in medical science, and a religious faith that said
there was hope—hope of release from their pain, hope of

cure, hope of a new life. As one of them said: "You just couldn't take this pain unless there was hope."

They were sharing in the fellowship of Paul's statement to the Galatian Christians about "bearing one another's burdens."

They were sharing experiences and entering into areas of life which only they knew and understood. Even their closest loved ones were shut out.

### Bearing One Another's Burdens

Despite many years of hospital ministry, of offering to others the comforting strength of God and the presence of Christ, the Great Physician, this experience of being shut out was strange to me and hard to understand.

But then I remembered. Those of us who must sit on the outside of that door, who cannot enter that room, also share a fellowship: those whom we love are in distress *and we would bear their burdens* . . . and we do! So we have a togetherness, too, albeit of a different kind.

Every child has heard and every parent has said, "This hurts me more than it does you." The child doesn't believe this, for he knows only the hurt of the punishment. But the parent suffers another kind of hurt—that emotion which never wants to see a loved one bear pain. He would gladly take it upon himself, if he could. I can now better grasp why David cried out: "Oh my son Absalom, my son, my son Absalom! would God I had died for thee!" (2 Sam. 18:33). Where true love is, there is the desire to take the hurt to oneself in order to protect the one who is **loved.**

I have felt wound, pain, and hurt in seeing my beloved

Ann walk her lonesome valley these past four years. Here
was a staggering blow from which one of weaker moral
fibre and Christian faith than she would have been mor-
tally wounded. This was not to say there was no recoil,
no flinching. There was! But, despite the blows, she stood,
firm and steadfast. The confidence of her surgeon that he
would win this battle, plus her own Christian faith, enabled her to stand.

Life is solo, in that each person must bear his own
burdens; but life is also chorus, in that, as Christians,
we share one another's burdens. Written across the pages
of the Bible, and thus planted deep in the structure of
the Christian life, is this principle of burden sharing. It
begins on the elemental level of sharing life's necessities,
and it climbs to the peak of spiritual sharing.

While it is true that we can help carry another's burdens, we can never carry another's responsibilities. There
are some roads we must walk alone.

As the spiritual says:

> Jesus walked this lonesome valley,
> He had to walk it by himself,
> Oh, nobody else could walk it for him,
> He had to walk it by himself.

Every life, soon or late, has burdens to bear. There are
those loads which come as a result of our own limitations,
lack of judgment, and poor planning. Most of these are
unnecessary, if we were but more careful.

There are some weights which come because we live in
an imperfect world, and situations arise over which we

have no control—disease, natural calamity, and the like. Some of these are inevitable.

Because of these, Christians feel that they must contribute something to the world other than the mere pulling of their own load; so they find themselves voluntarily assuming the cargo of others. All this, Paul says, is "fulfilling the compulsion of Christ."

### The Promise of God

Across the years I have faced, philosophically, the problems of pain and suffering. I have talked about it, preached about it, and written about it.[1] I have listened to those who have carried heavy yokes. And we have lived with it as a family these past three years. So I know that there is no easy, satisfactory answer. God's rain does fall on the just and on the unjust. So does drought. God's love and concern reach out to both the righteous and to the unrighteous. But, his sheep "hear his voice" and respond to that love. They know that concern, for they are close enough to hear, to feel, and to know.

I can in no way believe that disease is God's will. The very spelling of the word, *dis-ease*, indicates that it is not right. The will of God is that we have health. Oh, I suppose God is responsible even for the creation of disease germs. What their purpose is, I do not know. Maybe there is some reason or function for them which we do not as yet know. But I am firmly convinced and do believe this: God would never allow such a thing as cancer, or anything else, if *of itself* it had the power to defeat. I am also sure that the battle against disease *is* God's will, and I am grateful for all those who are taking part in this encounter.

Let us remember that Jesus did not say, "I have explained the world." He said, "I have overcome the world."

Across the years, I have come to believe that so long as a person can feel that he is loved at home, that he is loved by God, and that there is a meaning and purpose to life, he can take anything that life has to offer: failure, defeat, disappointment, business disaster, disease, calamity, *anything!* This I have preached and I am firmly convinced of its truth. It works!

Within each of us is that haunting fear that when life does rain its cruel blows upon us, we will not have the courage, faith, and fortitude to stand up under the crushing weight. It is not so much that we are afraid of the blows; rather, we are afraid that we will give way under them. But we can stand—if our foundation of life, love, and purpose is secure.

Let me close with one of the most marvelous assurances ever recorded of a faith that will hold us up and not let us go. It comes from one who felt life's lashes at their cruelest and yet called life a glorious adventure.

We have this treasure in earthen vessels, to show that the transcendent power belongs to God and not to us. We are afflicted in every way, but not crushed; perplexed, but not driven to despair; persecuted, but not forsaken; struck down, but not destroyed; always carrying in the body the death of Jesus, so that the life of Jesus may also be manifested in our bodies (2 Cor. 4:7–10, RSV).

Today's emphasis seems to be so much on the *vessel* that we have forgotten the treasure. But notice the emphasis Paul gives to the treasure:

*Afflicted, but not crushed.* Despite hardships and handicaps, there is no impasse on the road of God's will. Detours, perhaps, but no road closures. The way of God is not a dead end.

*Perplexed, but not driven to despair.* We are puzzled, but not despondent. It is the person who has no faith in God who comes to despair. Often where there is profound faith in God the perplexities increase, but there is never despair.

*Persecuted, but not forsaken.* We never have to stand alone. We may feel loneliness many times, but we are never completely alone.

*Struck down, but not discouraged.* We may be knocked down, more than once, but we are never knocked out! It is the mark of a champion in any sport that when he is knocked off his feet he gets up and goes on. That is why he is a champion. Paul concludes:

So we do not lose heart. Though our outer nature is wasting away, our inner nature is being renewed every day. For this slight momentary affliction is preparing for us an eternal weight of glory beyond all comparison, because we look not to the things that are seen but to the things that are unseen; for the things that are seen are transient, but the things that are unseen are eternal (2 Cor. 4:16, RSV).

### Notes

1. See author's "All Things Come Alike to All," *Preaching from Ecclesiastes* (Nashville: Broadman Press, 1958), p. 85.

# 4

## Journey to Jerusalem

### Luke 2:52; 24:48,52

Maxwell Anderson's drama, *Journey to Jerusalem,* was written and produced on Broadway when Adolph Hitler was at the height of his power and when his inhuman cruelty was at its worst. The theme of this prize-winning play was that religion is life's strongest bulwark against despair and chaos. It keeps life from coming apart at the seams. Man must be free to choose his own faith, but a faith he must have.

From the time of King David, Jerusalem has held a fascination for every faithful, devout Jew. To be buried on Mt. Zion was a dream to be fulfilled by only a select few. But to journey to Jerusalem! Ah, that was a dream to be realized. In the midst of Hitler's annihilation of some six million Jews, those followers of Judaism would greet each other at the end of the year with the poignant cry that they had used for centuries: "Next year, Jerusalem!"

Today there is that same feeling about Jerusalem, the Holy City, sacred to the followers of the world's three monotheistic religions: Judaism, Christianity, and Islam. The second holiest spot in the Islamic world is the Dome of the Rock Mosque in Jerusalem. Jews from seventy-three nations of the world make up the melting pot of modern Israel. And modern Jerusalem is a hostile, bitterly divided city. Muslims cannot go to one section, and Jews are forbidden to enter the other half. Each looks across a heavily guarded, strongly barricaded no man's land at places that are sacred to each. And it is an eerie feeling to walk those hundred yards or so called the Mandelbaum Gate, knowing that machine guns are trained on you from both directions.

Every Christian seems to have that strange compulsion to visit the Holy Land, to be able to do what Geoffrey O'Hara put into emotion-packed words in his song: "I walked today where Jesus walked,/And felt his presence there."

I have spent reverent days walking, studying, seeing, and thinking about this Jerusalem the Golden. It is amazing and almost unbelievable to see the changes that have been wrought by both Arabs and Jews in the past decade. That which for generations had been barren, rock-covered hills and heat-blistered desert is once again becoming a land of milk and honey. In Israel alone, more than fifty

million trees have been planted in the ten years since my
first visit.

In this chapter I want us to consider three visits that
Jesus made to his beloved city of Jerusalem. There is an
abiding lesson we can learn from these visits so that we
may apply them to our own cities. This lesson can furnish
us insight as to the place of the church in the destiny of
our cities. Each church must proclaim that its city is a
city about which Christ cares, even as he cared for Jerusalem.

### Dedication

The first of these visits we shall call the *journey of dedication*. It occurred when Jesus was eight days old, when
Mary and Joseph, in the tradition of their faith, brought
Jesus to the Temple for dedication to God. This was a
high act of worship, anchored in the ancient traditions of
their people, a tradition which Jesus would observe all
his life.

In the Gospel of Luke there is a striking phrase used
twice about Jesus: "*As his custom was,* he went into the
synagogue on the sabbath day" (4:16); and "He came out,
and went, *as was his custom,* to the Mount of Olives"
(22:39, RSV). In both cases, the custom had to do with
worship and prayer. Each time action was the inevitable
result. Instinctively and habitually Jesus worshiped
and prayed, not only in those solitary hours of personal
communion with God, but also in the hours of public
worship in God's house with God's people. For Jesus,
worship in church was as natural as "breathing out and
breathing in."

Why did Jesus have this habit? Nazareth was a small village inhabited by ordinary people; its reputation was unsavory. Nathanael had asked: "Can anything good come out of Nazareth?" (John 1:46, RSV). They even say it today about modern Nazareth, an Arab town in Israel. Besides, in Jesus' day there was no outstanding rabbi who would attract attention by his stimulating, exciting, and unusual interpretations of the Law. There was only an ordinary local rabbi doing his task. As one writer put it: "Jesus must have listened to an awful lot of drivel from the rabbis of his day."

The synagogue of Jesus' day was far from perfect. Jesus broke with many of its teachings. He criticized its weaknesses. He denounced the hollowness of many of its leaders. *But he believed in it.* Disagreement with the rabbis, criticisms of its weaknesses did not keep him from making participation in its worship a regular part of his life. When the sabbath came, Jesus was present for worship and instruction in the ways of God—*as was his custom.*

Worship is the way we have of keeping God central in our lives. And one is never too young to learn this. Jesus was brought to the Temple when he was only eight days old. I laughingly say to expectant mothers, "We will excuse you for one Sunday, if the baby is born in the middle of the week." But bringing the child to church at least insures the parents' presence, and the child sees from the beginning that the church is important to his parents.

It is often hard to keep our primary purposes in view when things of secondary value press in on every side. One night a teen-ager who had set up a priority list for the year's activities—church, school, athletics, and fraternity—

was discussing with his parents the lateness of his weekend hours. He had been up past midnight for three consecutive nights. Finally he exploded: "You just don't know the pressures I'm under. The other kids don't have it this way. I'm expected to be in church, at choir, get my lessons, be on the basketball court, and am fined if I'm not at fraternity functions. Everyone says I'm a leader, they're depending on me. I can't let 'em down. It's hard to keep everything going in the right order."

He was right. It is hard, and for adults, too. But I believe that the regular worship of God does help us to find the proper perspective. It did for one person, who said: "For me, regular attendance at the Sunday morning worship service has contributed more than its proportionate share to whatever spiritual development I've experienced. It has assured me of at least fifty-two hours a year given over to thoughts of God and his will for my life."

Worship each Sunday makes us sensitive to insights that are deeper than words. Robert Frost is said to have commented to a fellow poet that a poem begins with a lump in the throat. Well, that is what worship is: a lump in the throat, the deep feeling that gives direction to study and meaning to work. There is no substitute for regular worship in the church, despite good intentions of perhaps worshiping elsewhere.

A fellow pastor and I were talking about a revival that was being held in his church. (*Held* is too often the proper word, for the revival often doesn't break loose.) He said: "Avery, we've had people coming to church during this revival who haven't been to church in twenty years!"

Think of that: haven't been to church in twenty years!

Think what such a person has missed: the fellowship of God and all that it implies; the fellowship of Christian people, kindred minds; worship, singing, and inspiration; new developments at church; opportunities for finding out what life is all about and how to develop a Christian concept of living. It ought to be our custom, as it was Jesus', to be in church regularly, and to believe in its ability to carry out its functions.

### Enthusiasm

The second time Jesus went to Jerusalem was at the age of twelve years, when he entered the Temple to study and learn. We shall call this the *journey of enthusiasm*.

Every tourist who visits Jerusalem must feel excitement as he approaches the city, either from the air or coming up the winding road from Jericho. When he gets his first glimpse of that city set on a hill and sees the gleaming golden dome of the Dome of the Rock Mosque, he is bound to feel a quiver chase up his spine.

As a lad of twelve years, Jesus must have felt a great deal of excitement as he prepared for his journey. On this second visit, his parents were taking him to the city and the Temple for the religious observance called the Passover. It was on this occasion that Jesus got separated from his parents, and it was three days before they found him "in the temple, sitting among the teachers, listening to them and asking them questions (Luke 2:46, RSV).

His meeting with those learned rabbis must have been enthusiastic. There was something about this lad that produced an electrifying effect. Could it have been that some of those same rabbis who were so fascinated and capti-

vated by this boy of twelve years were the ones who so
violently turned against him twenty years later when he
was fulfilling the Father's business he so earnestly dis-
cussed with them?

We often assume that Jesus was doing the teaching on
that occasion. No doubt there is truth in this. Adults often
learn from children. However, the focus of this event is
in the fact that Jesus was there more as a learner than as
a teacher.

Having observed the sacred rituals of worship, Jesus
sat among the teachers, listening to them, asking questions,
and learning from them. All of us need to learn, to be
taught. The emotional quality that comes from worship
needs to be made secure by the mental quality of learning.
Worship without study could lead to superstition. The
Christian must move from the sanctuary to the classroom.

Unfortunately, some folk "sit among the teachers" *without* having observed the ritual of worship. They see worship and study as two of many activities a church offers,
from which they are free to choose. This is wrong. There
is little feeling for religious worship that is not based on
sound knowledge. There are people who go to church out
of a sense of duty or for the good feeling it gives them.
This is not enough. We need to be sure that our feelings
correspond with facts.

Jesus said: "I have come to bear witness to the truth."
That is the purpose behind education: the search for truth.
And no Christian should ever be afraid of that! The church
classroom invites the skeptic to raise his questions and the
doubter to express his doubts. It insists that people think.
The intellectual life of the church should match that found

on any college or university campus. There is no place in the church for closed minds. Like Jesus in the Temple, we must be found at the Father's business—listening, asking, and learning.

Too many adults have skipped the process of learning why they believe what they profess. Many college students, learning in every other area, overlook the importance of learning substantial reasons for their Christian faith. They never realize that others before them have doubted and have rid themselves of the encumbrances of childish beliefs—and without lessening their faith one whit! The church has a responsibility to be careful what it teaches so that it does not conflict with other areas of learning. Unnecessary tension arises when ideas have to be unlearned.

The church offers a place where one can listen, ask, and learn. A person should have the full assurance that in church, of all places, his views will be respected if not always accepted.

### Disillusion

This brings us to Jesus' third and last visit to Jerusalem, to enter the Temple for service. This visit is called "the triumphal entry," and the Christian calendar designates it as Palm Sunday. Let us call it the *journey of disillusion*.

Popular leaders often find enthusiastic followers gathered to greet them when they enter a city. I well remember the crowds in front of our church a few years ago when President Kennedy drove down St. Charles Avenue. And, what can compare with the spectacle of welcome when King Rex makes his annual New Orleans appearance on Mardi Gras Day? People shout approval without know-

ing why and praise the hero without being willing to support him. It is a familiar pattern of public reaction, and it
is just about what the so-called triumphal entry of Jesus
into Jerusalem amounted to: approval without knowledge,
praise without support.

Despite her beauty, Jerusalem can be terribly disillusion-
ing to today's visitor—the crass, open commercialism of
the Roman and Greek churches; the squabbles among
Christians over jurisdiction of sacred sites, so that for
centuries a Muslim has had to be "keeper of the keys" for
the Church of the Holy Sepulchre; St. Helena's recovery
of precious relics that were not lost. (If Jerusalem was
completely destroyed in the year A.D. 70, it puzzles me
how she found so many things two hundred years later.)
One visitor to the Holy Land put it this way: "I'm glad
I came; I wish I had never come."

It is easy for our youthful enthusiasms to give way to
disillusionment. Martin Luther, as a young monk, was
chosen for a visit to Rome. Already perplexed in his search
for biblical truth, he approached the visit with enthusiasm,
hoping his search would be rewarded. But his disappointment was climaxed as he climbed the "Scala Sancta" at St.
John's in Lateran on his knees. He saw beneath the surface
and got to his feet. The truth of the New Testament—"the
just shall live by faith—" took on new significance for the
entire world.

When Jesus came to Jerusalem that last time, he headed
straight for the Temple, the center and symbol of religious
life and of his personal life. Neither threatened opposition
nor demonstrated acclaim could deter him from his purpose. "He entered Jerusalem . . . and went into the tem-

ple." And he was disillusioned by what he saw: money changers who had turned the place of prayer into a den of thieves; sheep, cattle, and pigeons that made the place look like a livestock pavilion; travellers who used the Temple as a shortcut across the city.

## Education—Action

There are two ways to respond to disillusionment: with cynicism, which throws the baby out with the bath; or with consecration, which triggers off constructive action. Jesus chose the latter course. He overturned the tables, drove out the money changers, and dispersed the livestock. Then came the more constructive action: the sick were healed, the children were cared for, and a great lesson on sacrificial giving was learned from the widow who gave her mite. Day after day during this last week, Jesus used his energy in constructive action.

A mere crusading spirit is not enough. Action must be matched with consecration and dedication to the will of God. Is what is being done worth dying for? More important, is it worth living for? Is it worth one's wholehearted allegiance and commitment? There are jobs to be done, and Christians should be doing them: classes to be taught, youth groups to counsel, visits to be made, barriers of racial antagonism to be melted, money needed to support the church and its missions, hundreds of things to be done. And every Christian should be doing something.

Jesus believed in worship, but worship alone is not enough: "Not every one who says to me, 'Lord, Lord,' shall enter the kingdom of heaven, but he who does the will of my father who is in heaven" (Matt. 7:21, RSV).

Jesus believed in education, but learning by itself is insufficient: "Every one then who hears these words of mine and does them will be like a wise man" (v. 24).

We come to this, then: Jesus' three trips to the Temple illustrate three facts of the Christian life: worship, study, and service. All are important, but none is complete without the others.

Worship without study degenerates into superstition; without work it becomes empty formalism.

Study without worship loses its vitality; without work it becomes hypocritical—and hypercritical.

Work without worship is drudgery; without study it is meaningless.

I emphasize this because people frequently substitute one of these for all three of them. One person attends worship but is involved in no constructive study or service. Another is stimulated by the discussions but has never learned to worship or work. Someone else is an activist, always at work, but never involved in worship or study. Such limitations are really heresy. To treat a portion of the gospel as if it were the whole gospel is to miss the gospel. A partial faith is not enough.

It is easy to mistake the *reward* of Christian living for the *goal* of Christian faith. That "fellowship," for example, or "peace of mind"—these may be by-products, but never the goal of Christian faith. Let us not equate them. True, there are those who come to church because they are lonely, and they find friends. Some come because they are distressed, and they find inner peace. But fellowship sought as a goal soon sours, and one whose pursuit is peace of mind is heading for anxiety. Such things evaporate quickly when sought as goals or used as ends or made the chief purpose of church.

An engineering friend of mine points out that the triangle is the principle of all construction. Any square or rectangle will change its shape under pressure unless it is braced. The triangle gives support. The basics of Christian living form a triangle to lend us sound support: worship, study, and service. Or, to say it another way: soul, mind, body. Or, heart, brain, and hand. It makes little difference how you say it; it means the same thing. This trilogy is so built into life that it comes out the same.

I suppose that all I am saying could be symbolized by the very structure of our church buildings. The sanctuary is the focal point, symbolizing the centrality of worship. The educational facilities surround it, symbolizing the importance of learning and providing worship with a strong foundation. Our entrances and exits lead us as Christians out from worship and study into the pathways of life we are to serve. Thus, the very physical structure of our church buildings symbolize the three trips of our Lord to the Temple: once to worship, another time to learn, and the last for service. Those same three trips are to be ours.

After telling of the burial of Jesus, the resurrection, the post-resurrection appearances, and the final farewell, Luke concludes his narrative by saying that the disciples "returned to Jerusalem with great joy, and were continually in the temple blessing God" (24:52–3). Continually in the temple! Let that be our story, as twentieth-century disciples of Christ.

# 5

## Christ in the Midst of the Church

### Matthew 18:20

When we use the term *church,* we must explain what is
meant, for people have so many different conceptions of
what is meant by the church that in discussions we do not
all start from the same premise. (See chapter 1, p. 14.)

Some think of the church as being a specific denominational group—the Roman Catholic Church, the Greek
Orthodox, the Methodist, or the Baptist church. Yes, I
know, most Baptists say there is no such thing as "the
Baptist church"; there are only Baptist churches. To me,
that is quibbling over semantics. If a group of people hold
certain things in common, then they should be considered
not only as churches, but also as a church.

Others look upon the church as being a specific local congregation, saying that this is the most often used description in the New Testament. And it is.

A few even think of the church as being the building itself and that religion is what goes on inside that building. They too often feel that they can leave their religion inside the building when the services are over, forgetting that service on the outside is a natural outgrowth of worship on the inside.

In the deepest sense, however, there is only one church, and it is composed of all who believe in and accept Jesus Christ as Saviour and Lord of life. This is what the New Testament calls "the body of Christ."

The definition of a church generally accepted by Baptists says, "The church is an organized body of baptized believers." This is rather good, but it is inadequate. The *real church* is composed of all believers. There must be an organization to promote and spread that belief, as well as to provide a fellowship of those believers. The church needs baptism as an open testimony or declaration of the believer's acceptance and commitment to Christ.

### Where Two or Three

Looking at the text, "Where two or three are gathered in my name, there am I in the midst of them," we get another idea of the church. Wherever believers in Christ are gathered, there is the church, and Christ is in the midst of that church.

The early Christians really felt that Jesus Christ was truly in their midst. They relied upon his presence for guidance and inspiration. They were dictated to by the

Spirit of Christ so that their actions had his endorsement.
They did not act and then interpret their actions as being
his, as we are so prone to do. They first sought to be so in
harmony with Christ's spirit that their actions would then
be like his had been.

We are gathered in any service of worship as a fellowship of believers in Christ. Not all of us think exactly
alike, not even all of us who belong to some particular
expression of the church. Usually not all are even members of the same denomination. Perhaps not all are believers in Christ, for that matter. But we are gathered,
for the most part, around our common belief, seeking for
the kind of action that would be worthy of the sanction of
Christ. Gathering in a service of worship is for the purpose of praising and giving thanks to God, to be sure. But
worship should, and must, produce lives outside the worship that demonstrate that we have been in the presence
of God. In other words, our belief is to be matched with
our behavior.

So, I want us to look at the church which has Christ in
its midst. The method is to try and picture Christ in company with some believers and unbelievers of his day and
see the parallel for our day. There shall be three major
divisions: (1) Christ in the midst of the church asking
and answering questions; (2) Christ in the midst of the
church in its sorrow, pain, and sin; (3) Christ in the midst
of the church's triumph.

### Jesus' Questions

One of the first glimpses of Jesus that we have is on the
occasion when he was about twelve years old. His family

had gone to Jerusalem for the Passover. When they started home, they left Jesus behind. After a day's journey to the village just north of Jerusalem, now called Beeri, they returned to Jerusalem to look for him. They found Jesus in the Temple, "seated among the teachers, listening to them and asking them questions, till all his hearers were amazed at the intelligence of his own answers" (Luke 2:46–47, Moffatt).

When his parents asked why he had behaved so, he turned to them with a question: "Why did you look for me? Did you not know that I had to be at my Father's house, doing my Father's business?" (author's paraphase)

From that point, Jesus' ministry was characterized by his asking and answering questions, questions concerning the ways of God with men, of men with God, and of men with one another.

In talking about John the Baptist, he asked: "What did you go out into the wilderness to see? A prophet? A reed shaken in the wind? What did you expect?"

In trying to get the disciples to know who he was he asked: "Who do men say that I am?" Always Jesus emphasized the personal response.

In his conversation with Nicodemus, he asked if Nicodemus could explain either the wind or physical birth. Then he pointed out the mystery of the new birth that brought new life.

David A. MacLennan suggests some questions that Jesus might ask of us:

Why have you so little faith in God? in your fellow man? in yourself? Why don't you do what is right? Why do you think the Christian basis for action is nonsense in this kind of world? Why doesn't your "religionless Christianity" or "God-is-dead" philosophy give you more joy?

Dr. MacLennan goes on to say:

The late Halford E. Luccock had an inimitable sermon on this theme. (*Marching Off the Map,* Harpers, 1952). "Hal" was sure that when Jesus asked questions he was pushing his attack into the opponent's corner, a strategy of tremendous value, and all too often neglected. When opponents put their difficult and sometimes damning questions to Christians, we ought to be able to come back as our Lord did: "I will also ask you a question." [1]

There are some in today's church, unfortunately, who do not want to ask questions or seek answers. Some cannot stand the strain of possibly learning that they may be wrong, or that at most they have only partial answers. They are afraid of any new truth that might rearrange their neat little patterns. One outstanding pastor said in my presence, "I never read these new books. They might disturb my faith." What kind of faith is that? A faith that cannot stand questioning is not worth having. We are not supposed to hold up our faith: our faith is to hold us up. Too long has the church failed to awaken the intellect and curiosity of man. And if it does not, it will fail, for man is by nature curious.

Others do not ask questions because they already have the answers; they can learn nothing more. Of course, some of the answers may be to things people are not interested in knowing, or have already outgrown. Such people try to use yesterday's answers for today's questions. And many would rather face yesterday's questions. What shallow vessels to be so easily filled. More important and more pathetic, by being satisfied with so little, they miss out on the fuller knowledge and blessing of God.

### Experiment in Change

All groups are interested in youth. Each denomination has its equivalent counterpart of the Baptist Training Union. Despite the demonstrated values of the Training Union and the constant efforts toward its improvement, the Training Union is one of the two units of Baptist organizational life most difficult to maintain. (The Brotherhood is the most difficult.)

Our high school Training Union group took a novel approach. Under the guidance of the church's youth director, they began with the music of today's youth. Instead of despairing about its loud, raucous beat, they decided to go into the "whys" of this music. Why did it appeal? What was its message, if any?

The "Top Forty" tunes were taken from the local rating sheets and each member was asked to list his own ten favorites. Out of these, the top ten were chosen for discussion and analysis. Records and record player were secured and the words were mimeographed. On given evenings the records were played, the words were read, then there was discussion about the significance of the appeal. Efforts were made to see if there were any ethical, moral, or theological implications, or if there was any carry-over of the music's ideas into life.

For example, one of the most popular records dealt

with the theme of the death of a young lover and the resultant sadness. In the discussion, it was revealed that the youth present did not consider any Christian concept of death, immortality, or eternal life because of this record. Most thought of it in terms of some sort of "possible reunion," but that was about all. As a result, there came an excellent opportunity for enlargement of the Christian doctrine and teachings concerning eternal life with God.

One of the most popular local disc jockeys was invited for one meeting. He had never been around a church group and was enthralled with the idea. After a good presentation of the technical aspects of the recording industry, he got into the "ethics of payola" (indirect payment for a commercial favor such as plugging a record). He frankly confessed that at one point in his career he had been a full participant. Unfortunately, he saw no moral involvement and he had ceased merely because he feared for his career. The subsequent discussion did afford an excellent chance to talk about ethical and moral principles to be followed by Christians both in school and business.

This particular emphasis climaxed with a Sunday evening presentation of music with the modern youth beat. It was not as "far out" as originally planned, for both the youth director and the pastor got cold feet and modified the music. However, a Beatle-type music group of high schoolers playing guitars, drums, and string bass did accompany both the congregational singing and the choir numbers.

The congregation was educated in advance as to what to expect. A Wednesday night service was used to explain and prepare the older folk for what was to happen. On the night of this service, attendance was as large as on Sunday morning. The music was well received, and the idea was appreciated. One young guitar player refused to participate, feeling it was sacrilegious. And his feelings were respected. One adult commented, "This isn't new. I grew up on such music out in West Texas churches." And another said, "What's so modern about this? We still sing this way in many parts of Missouri."

A Jewish newspaperman gave the service full news coverage, with pictures. Many requests from other churches were received, wanting to know how to do it. And one church even used its paper to editorialize "against" such a procedure.

Out of this grew the desire for a music service for other age groups. A service is now being designed featuring people aged sixty and above singing the music they sang in church when they were young. This music and its message will also be interpreted for religious significance. One woman in her seventies, formerly a trained musician, has agreed to solo. This calls for educating the youth as to what to expect and reminding them that her voice was once one of the best. The music of the adult world, especially that of older adults, has little appeal to youth, just as adult ideas and standards are rejected by youth. But orginially this was the music and these were the ideas of youth.

### The Right Questions

Professor John Killinger of Vanderbilt tells of an exchange between Archibald MacLeish and George Buttrick, when Buttrick was preacher at Harvard's Memorial Church. After first declining Dr. Buttrick's invitation to conduct morning prayers, MacLeish accepted but made his position clear: "I'm not at all convinced that Christianity has the answers we're looking for—but I do think it has the right questions." [2]

Too long have certain elements of the church been intolerant. An intolerant church is a contradiction in terms, whether it expresses its intolerance in the dogma of the Roman Catholics, the fervor of the fundamentalists, or the conceit of the modernists.

Modern Roman Catholicism, despite its use of the term "separated brethren" and its new pronouncement on religious liberty, still harbors the arrogant claim that other Christians are living in error. This church must face the humility of the Christ who washed his disciples' feet and who countered all totalitarian claims of monopoly by saying, "Other sheep have I which are not of this fold." Fundamentalists must see that without a full commitment of mental capacity and social compassion they can never enduringly be effective. And modern Protestantism no longer directs the patterns of life. It has lost its driving power. Its dull conformity is neither hot nor cold but is alarmingly tepid, as was the church at Laodicea. Efficient in the mechanics of organization, it is sadly deficient in spiritual warmth, and dull in its concern.

Just to ask questions is not enough. We must ask the right questions. What good does it do to have answers that are unimportant? Some questions may not have answers at all, certainly not easy ones. But we cannot evade asking them; we must try to find some answer.

We must ask questions about modern warfare—about Viet Nam and the Dominican Republic, about napalm bombs, nuclear testing, atomic fallout and its influence on unborn generations. What about corruption in high places and the general decline in morality? And what about racial discrimination? This is a problem we all must face. In the fellowship of Christ there is no such thing as distinction, for in Christ there is no East, West, South, or North—neither Jew nor Greek, male nor female, Negro nor white, Caucasian nor Oriental.

The economic phase of life has its issues. The jurisdictional strikes between unions do not aid the cause of the laborer. And the planned obsolescence of today's manufacturer, with its resultant waste of natural resources, is sinful.

We must face our large church membership, big budgets, and great buildings with our low influence as seen in the rising crime rate, increased alcoholism, and breakdown of the home. Our preaching must be matched with our practice. How can we justify ourselves in producing a Charles Van Doren, a Billie Sol Estes, or a Bobby Baker? We cannot ignore the price fixing of General Electric, nor the violence of the Teamster's Union, nor the irresponsibility of a New York Transit strike, nor the danger in a Watts rebellion.

Yes, today's Christianity does ask "right questions." They may not be asked in the sharp eloquence of scriptural language, but the questions are asked: Who am I? Does life have any meaning? Any purpose? Is there any responsibility for anyone other than oneself? Should we get involved with the problems and troubles of others?

Why not scrap the old morality for a "new morality"? Is Jesus Christ necessary for a working faith?

The church that does not ask questions is walking oblivion road. It cannot endure. It is already in retreat. Every generation must answer its own questions. And each generation can depend upon Christ being in its midst to help. You see, the church does not represent unchanging certainty. Rather, the church represents an open-ended search for God's will in our lives as his eternal truth is applied to our lives.

The only unchanging certainty the church has is the reality of God.

### The Sorrow of the Church

In the second place, Christ is in the midst of the sorrow, pain, and sin of the church.

We see this most clearly at the time of the arrest, trial, and crucifixion of Christ. There the deepest sorrow, the most intense pain, and the blackest sin met. But through all the ministry of Jesus, we see him going where human need is most acute. At Jacob's well with the Samaritan woman, in the meeting with Zaccheus, at the coming of the man sick with palsy and the woman taken in adultery, at the death of Lazarus—in all these episodes Jesus was meeting needs, healing diseases, binding up the wounds of the brokenhearted, and restoring the wayward with a forgiving love.

The church is the battleground where we must face a world that has lost its way and is causing unbearable suffering, pain, and misery in its stumbling, staggering search. But too often the church is interested in distant sorrow and sin while it lacks compassion for those close at hand.

We are keen on foreign missions. And rightly so. But let us not be insensitive to our backyard neighbors. In sending missionaries to Africa, South America, and the Orient we do right. But let us not forget that we have Negroes, Latin Americans, and Orientals in our own church neighborhood.

Our offerings for foreign missions exceed what we do for home missions, which are in turn larger than what we give to state missions. Even those who say that "missions begin at home" forget to match their sentiment with their dollars.

The church must minister to individual needs of distress and pain. But does it? Do we as its members? Do I as a pastor? And I must confess my own shortcomings at this point. There are shut-ins who are neglected, retired people who are overlooked, youth not given adult leadership, and sinners who are left alone. Sometimes we are negligent because we just do not know the people and the situation. Often we are busy with other things equally important. Then there are those times when we are just plain negligent.

So many of us, when it comes to doing something, merely content ourselves with a bit of prayer. Let us remember that prayer is not necessarily crying aloud to God for help. Sometimes you just cannot cry aloud. Prayer is more often an inner response, a quiet talk with God, the pouring out of one's deepest feelings. Then there comes that quiet confidence that sends us out in boldness to face whatever we must face.

I like the story Paul Scherer relates of the little girl at the weekend party who was found one morning in such deep distress that she was asked what was the matter. "Somebody," she moaned, pointing to the bushes that lined the garden path, and brushing the tears from her eyes, "Somebody has gone and set traps out there for the birds." "And what have you done about it?" "I have prayed about it," she answered. "I have prayed that none of the birds would go near the traps!" Then a long pause, and a sob. "And I have prayed that if any did, the traps would not work!" Another long pause, and another sob, though not so bitter now. "And just a few minutes ago," she went on, looking up through her tears and smiling, "I went out there and kicked the traps to pieces." [3]

Ah, there is Christ in the midst of sorrow, pain, and sin: not just praying about it, *but doing something about it!*

Who knows the problems, burdens, and tears that are hidden by everyday smiles? Who knows the grief that is compensated for by an aggressiveness which is just seeking some small measure of affection? If we but knew, perhaps we could do more than pray; *we could help!* We do have the responsibility to learn where there is a burden we can lift or a tear we can wipe dry, for that is the example of Christ. The Scriptures tell us to "bear one another's burdens." With Christ in our midst, we can.

It would be distressed loneliness to face some of the bludgeonings of life without the mutual support that comes from faith in God and concerned friends. I know what it is to receive such support, and I know how people come to me with problems I never dreamed they had, saying, "Somehow, I think you will understand."

### Christ and Triumph

The greatest triumph was the defeat of death in Christ's resurrection. The sun had gone down on that Friday as the darkest tragedy of history unfolded. But the sun rose the following Sunday morning on the brightest triumph of eternity. In the midst of that tragedy and triumph we see Jesus. Listen to some of the things said about him:

"I find no fault in him."

"Surely, this man was the Son of God."

"This same Jesus whom you see go away will come again."

"He is not here. He is risen!"

Christ had won! And if those early Christians would abide in his truth, they would win, too.

There are those today who say the church is in danger. One writes:

The Church is like a ship on whose deck festivities are still kept up and glorious music is heard, while deep below the water-line a leak has sprung and masses of water are pouring in, so that the vessel is settling hourly lower though the pumps are manned day and night.[4]

Of course the church is in danger! It was meant to be in danger. If the church is not in danger it is not functioning properly, and if it is not functioning properly it deserves to be in danger for another reason. But the church is not doomed! The church as we know it may pass away. But the church Christ established will remain.

When Jesus said that the gates of hell would not be able to prevail against the church, maybe you thought he meant that hell was making the assault. Not so! It was the church that was storming the gates of hell, and those gates could not hold out, he said.

Well, the Christian faith has never had an easy time of it. It was never promised an easy time. Jesus told his followers: "In the world ye shall have tribulation: but be of good cheer; I have overcome the world" (John 16:33). The normal thing for the church and the Christian is tribulation. Why are we so surprised when it comes? The emphasis of Jesus is not on the tribulation, but on *triumph!*

The future does not look rosy for the church. Already outnumbered better than two to one, the birthrate of Christian converts every year lags behind the physical birthrate. Numerically, we lose ground every day. The road ahead is rocky and steep. But we must not succumb to pessimism nor stand idly by and let the critics of the church go unchallenged.

I believe in the church, for the light of God has shined in the darkness, and the darkness cannot put it out. I believe that Jesus was right in saying the gates of hell cannot prevail against his advancing church. *But, that church must advance.* It cannot sit still, it cannot rest on past laurels, it cannot keep its voice silent. It must meet terribly complex issues. Before it can offer answers, it must know the questions. The church must speak and it must act by applying what it does know of Christian ideals and principles to what it knows are acute problems of human relationships.

### Never Defeat

The Bible knows nothing of the word defeat as applied to the church. Hardship? Yes. Opposition? Yes. But defeat? *Never!* Jesus described the church as a conquering force. That early church had its faults and its weaknesses. But it was a mighty force for God. Despite the opposition of Roman force, Jewish antagonism, and Greek intellectualism, the early church met its opponents head on!

Today's church, including our own, is not perfect. It has plenty of faults. None of us as its members are what we ought to be, what we know we ought to be, or even what we want to be. But we do love Christ and we are committed to his cause. We can change our world, even as that earlier world was changed. It may take a long time. It took three hundred years to take hold of Rome.

The book of the Revelation was written on this theme. Tragedy, persecution, and death threatened the life of the church in its infancy. But that threatened church triumphed over its enemies.

No cause is worth living or dying for until someone has lived and died to make it worth living and dying for. Christ loved the church and gave himself for it—*i.e.*, for the believers who made up the church—and thus he made the church itself worth living and dying for.

Who knows what tragedy we may be called upon to face? What does it matter what threatens us? Christ is in the midst of the church, and it will be the church triumphant! But, will we be a part of that triumph? Some will; some will not.

My chief concern is not for the ultimate triumph of the church. I believe in that. Nor am I concerned about the ultimate triumph of righteousness. I believe in that, too, for God is righteous, and God will not be defeated. Nothing that is morally wrong—slavery, prejudice, war, racial

discrimination, economic injustice, people in starvation
and bondage,—none of these can prevail forever. *They
must go!* And they will.

My concern is that I and my generation shall somehow
miss out on being used by these ideas of justice, equality,
sharing, and righteousness that are embodied in Jesus
Christ, and are thus to be embodied in his followers, the
church. I am concerned that some of you should miss out.
And I am concerned lest our church miss out, too.

Christ is in the midst of the church: *thinking*—asking
and answering life's questions; *working*—coming to grips
with life's sorrows, pain, and sin; *giving*—loving the
church and giving himself for it so that the church will
emerge in triumph.

### Notes

1. David A. MacLennan, "Pulpit Patterns," *The Pulpit,* June,
1966, p. 28.

2. John Killinger, *The Thickness of Glory* (New York: Abing-
don Press, 1965), pp. 91–92.

3. Paul Scherer, *The Word God Sent* (New York: Harper &
Row, 1966), p. 89.

4. Karl Heim, *Christian Faith and Natural Science* (New
York: Harper & Bros., 1953), p. 24.

# 6

## A Redemptive Alternative

### Zephaniah 10:8–10

Evil is visible on every hand, and naturally we must be realistic in our appraisals of where we stand in regard to our practice of Christianity. We do often fall far short in the practice of what we profess. But if evil is all we can hope for or expect from human beings, we might as well give up right now. Rather than become absorbed in pessimism concerning the future of the church or the world, we should be emphasizing the possibilities of good within us.

One of the great recurring themes of the Bible is the

81

doctrine of the remnant. By definition, *remnant* means a piece or a part of the whole, something that remains, that is left over. It can be either useless or useful. Much is made in the Old Testament of the remnant idea. God would have spared Sodom could he have found but ten righteous men. He reduced Gideon's forces to three hundred men of resolute initiative. It is God's method to start and carry forward his purposes with minorities—often a minority of one!

### The Prophets' Message

Most of the Old Testament prophets speak on this theme of "the left ones," the remnant. Isaiah says that a remnant shall be saved, but that even that remnant shall itself pass through fire: " 'And though a tenth remain in it, it will be burned again, like a terebinth or an oak, whose stump remains standing when it is felled.' The holy seed is in the stump" (Isa. 6:13, RSV).

Micah's writing says that the scattered remnant will be reunited in Palestine and again become one flock as in the days of Saul, David, and Solomon. But Micah's remnant is bent on revenge. (See 5:8–15.) Every enemy is to be confronted and destroyed. The destruction is to be complete: armies, cities, forts, and shrines. This is not "an eye for an eye," but ten eyes for one eye, ten teeth for one tooth. What a striking contrast between this "son of vengeance" and the Sermon on the Mount.

Zephaniah says: "The remnant . . . shall not do iniquity, nor speak lies. They shall trust in the name of the Lord" (Zeph. 3:13,12).

Here is a rebuke of the proud and a promise for the

humble. God alone can provide security. God alone is strong. God alone controls the world.

Zechariah points out that one third of the nation will survive, but it will be a remnant out of which God will forge a new community, dedicated and conformed to his will.

In each of the prophetic writings there seem to be three steps that each prophet speaks about: (1) *apostasy,* man's sin and disobedience to God; (2) *doom,* a time of purification, not annihilation; (3) *remnant,* a small group which shall lead the return to God. This could be illustrated with two funnels placed next to each other—broad to narrow to broad.

Each prophet has an unshakable faith and a confidence in the power of God. No situation is ever completely without hope. God is never without a redemptive alternative. This, to me, would be the fuller meaning of the term remnant—*a redemptive alternative.*

One of the most provocative and influential writers on today's scene is a martyred twentieth-century German named Dietrich Bonhoeffer. I first became acquainted with him through a little book purchased on a bargain counter, entitled *Life Together,* which was a discussion of the Christian fellowship. Bonhoeffer, a German Lutheran pastor, was put to death in one of Hitler's earliest concentration camps. His writings came largely while he was imprisoned and have become significant two decades after his death.

In *Life Together* he says:

It is not simply to be taken for granted that the Christian has the privilege of living among other Christians. Jesus Christ lived in the midst of his enemies. At the end all his disciples deserted him. On the Cross he was utterly alone, surrounded by evildoers and mockers. . . . "I will sow them among the people: and they shall remember me in far countries" (Zech. 10:9). According to God's will Christendom is a scattered people, scattered like seed "into all the kingdoms of the earth" (Deut. 28:25). God's people must dwell in far countries among the unbelievers, but it will be the seed of the Kingdom of God in all the world.

"I will . . . gather them; for I have redeemed them: . . . and they shall turn" (Zech. 10:8–9). When will that happen? It has happened in Jesus Christ, who died that "he should gather together in one the children of God that were scattered abroad" (John 11:52), and it will finally occur visibly at the end of time when the angels of God "shall gather together his elect from the four winds, from one end of heaven to the other" (Matt. 24:31). Until then, God's people remain scattered, held together solely in Jesus Christ, having become one in the fact that, dispersed among unbelievers, they remember *Him* in the far countries.[1]

I suppose a good summary of this Old Testament thinking is found in Isaiah 36:4–7, which describes the situation just before the fall of Jerusalem in 586 B.C. An invading army was at the gates of the city and one of the enemy generals, Rabshakeh, was challenging the people in their own language. This is as fine a piece of psychological warfare as history ever recorded. What he said was so unanswerable and so calculated to break down the resistance of the Hebrew people that their leaders asked him to stop speaking Hebrew and use Aramaic instead.

No charge could have been more devastating than when General Rabshakeh sarcastically charged that these Hebrew people were relying on religion. He said: "What a mockery, to expect help from the God you have banished

. . . you fool nobody but yourselves, parading your faith in a God whom by your own action you have disowned." (author's paraphrase) And there was nothing they could say, for it was true. They did have a name for worshiping Jehovah. But in this crisis, instead of turning to Jehovah their God, they had put their trust in the horses and chariots of Egypt.

### Modern Gods

But what of us today? Dare we criticize them? We have claimed to be Christian. We have so labeled our civilization. We have so characterized our own nation. There have even been bills before our Congress that would by legislation officially declare the United States to be a Christian nation. Some other people might ask us if anything characteristically Christian has marked our efforts to solve domestic and international problems. And I believe we could answer that some definitely Christian efforts have been made.

Nevertheless, a modern Rabshakeh would charge: "You are Christian in name, and Christian in conduct when it suits you, and for the rest of the time you play the world's game according to the world's rules."

And we cannot evade that challenge. Our trust is not really in God. It is in guided missiles, space ships, nuclear bombs, and the like. We trust in North Atlantic Treaty Organizations and Southeast Asia Treaty Organizations. Speak as we may of the influence of Christianity for good, we have not yet produced a social order that is fully Christian in its emphasis or spirit.

A few years ago the International Missionary Council

met in what was then the world's newest nation, Ghana. At this meeting Prime Minister Kwame Nkrumah of Ghana spoke. He spoke of the new nation that was being built. He warned that the task would be beyond them if all the groups—religious, racial, and tribal—which made up Ghana insisted on their separateness and underlined what divided them instead of the truths and purposes which held them together. The Prime Minister said to those world Christian leaders:

All of you are here from different nations, different religious professions, but nevertheless you are met together in common concern and charity. But how can there be goodwill if Christians think more of their differences than of their whole-hearted devotion to the God of all above? How can the Christian message be spread effectively to the hopeful and inquiring masses of Africa, if it does not come to them rooted in that charity which is the bond of perfection?

Then the Prime Minister indicated that he did not have too much to encourage him as he looked abroad.

We see vast wealthy nations pouring out their tremendous treasure on sterile arms. We see powerful peoples engaged in a futile and destructive armament race. We see precious capital that might help raise up Africa and Asia flung away on potential destruction. What has this to do with Christian charity proclaimed by the West, or by the human brotherhood we hear so much about from the East? Seen from the angle of Africa's needs and hopes, the rivalry of the great powers looks like one thing only—a senseless, fratricidal struggle to destroy the very substance of humanity.[2]

Hearing such beautiful words, one could wish that Nkrumah had heeded his own advice.

This statement is but one of many that have come from the leaders of the new nations of the world. It ought to give us concern. And there are plenty of concerned voices being raised, some of them filled with portents of doom that would do credit to the weeping Jeremiah.

Some remind us that we are in spiritual decline, that we have neglected our Christian heritage, and that we have gone whoring after the false gods of money, security, ease, and pleasure. Others show us that despite our numerical signs of religiosity, there is no evidence of a sweeping repentance and faith, no decisive change of heart and life. So the claim is made that we are spiritually second-rate.

I am neither a prophet, nor the son of a prophet, but I do believe that if we would realistically face the facts of life in today's America—today's New Orleans, today's St. Charles Avenue Baptist Church, our own personal lives —we would find more than enough evidence that would justify the same voice of concern declared by those Old Testament prophets. Despite increased church membership, buildings, and finances, we find that right is too often decided by majority opinion, dictated by expediency, or caused by the ring of the cash register. We find that there is an infatuation with popular approval—consensus thinking. We find that absolute principles have given way to relative standards.

Broadway measures success by the length of the run, rather than the content of the show. Television renews contracts on the basis of ratings and audience polls. Sexual morality pays more attention to Kinsey reports than it does to biblical teaching and the proved experiences of family life. What is popular is considered to be right. The code of conformity snares individuals into mass thinking. Loyalty to society is put ahead of loyalty to God. Detachment of responsibility from the will of God has led to a vanishing of all sense of responsibility to God. As a result, many are claiming that American culture is becoming mediocre.

One danger of our day is that we have become so accustomed to the gospel of Jesus Christ that we miss its revolutionary character. Our familiarity has bred a sort of contempt. Modern psychology confirms the claim that minds which are continually subjected to either an appeal or a warning which they propose not to hear, develop a fatal immunity to truth. We have had both appeals and warnings, and we have heeded neither.

There are two ways of evaluating the present stage of development in either a person or a society:

First, to view the distance already covered, which is good, but which has a tendency toward contentment. Second, to see the distance yet to be covered, which should cause unrest. And most of us do not want to be disturbed.

The prophets counseled complete trust in God, but they also gave rise to a holy impatience when they were asked to dwell in a halfway house.

### The New Testament Remnant

In the New Testament, Paul revives the idea of the remnant. Despite the rough conditions of the time, Paul indicates that one cannot say that God has rejected his people so long as there is a remnant in the church. Paul's idea is that God selects his special agents from the entire group, choosing them without regard to their merit. This does not mean that God takes no account of their suitability. It means that no one earns the right because of previous virtue. Anyone and everyone is *chosen by grace,* God's grace!

Of the many examples Paul could have chosen, he decided to use the prophet Elijah. Dispirited and apparently defeated, this man of God convinced himself that he was the sole supporter of a cause now ruined. Actually, as God pointed out to Elijah, he was only one of seven thousand who stood firm.

The story of Elijah is a classic example of a pessimism which rests on judgments based on appearances. Even when the outlook may seem to justify despair, there are signs, if recognized, of unfaltering purpose.

Then Paul goes on to say that although the church may be small, provided it is faithful to its vocation it will not be insignificant. This confidence is founded upon the conviction that the redemption of the many will come through the service of the few.

We can see this truth illustrated in national statistics: although 95 percent of our citizens say they believe in God, only some 65 percent belong to any church or synagogue, and only 33 percent of these attend their church regularly.

The promises of God had come to all of the people of Israel, but the nation had never risen to the full height of its privilege and responsibility. At every period only a devoted minority accepted the appointed task and faith-

fully served God. It was the nucleus which was always
the saving element. In spite of the apostasy of the many,
the sacrifice of the few kept alive a devotion to the will of
God. Sometimes this minority of the redemptive dwindled
so that there seemed to be only one person. In fact, the
remnant finally was perfectly expressed in the one known
as "the Suffering Servant." And ultimately this Servant was
identified as Jesus of Nazareth.

But, having been narrowed to a single personality,
perfectly obedient to the will of God, the remnant was
now capable of indefinite expansion through the church,
through which the will of God in Christ was to work itself.
The funnel had narrowed; now it began to broaden. Beginning with the "economy of twelve," expanding to sev-
enty "sent ones," finally the church was looked upon as a
committed company of believers.

### A Modern Remnant?

To me a more important question than either the necessity or the possibility of another remnant in our time
is this: Am I willing and able to be a part of the remnant
if it does become necessary? Or would I be one who would
conform to the larger whole?

I honestly do not know! And neither do you. I believe
that I would, and I pray God and trust God that my faith
is the kind that would have the strength and courage to
answer affirmatively. But remember, Peter proclaimed
that even if everyone else would deny Jesus, *he* would
remain loyal. Yet, in a matter of mere hours, Peter had
denied with curses any knowledge of the man Jesus.
Peter's denial came, not because of lack of physical cour-

age, for Peter was never afraid physically. But he could not take the taunts and ridicule of his fellows, which requires more courage than to face physical danger. Yet, Peter later found the inner power which enabled him to become stalwart in his faith.

Who knows but that the twentieth-century church may be called upon to play that role? And who knows which of us would be able to meet the qualifications of the remnant?

There might be ground for the deepest despair concerning today's church, except for one thing: "The characteristic mode of the church's existence is death and resurrection." [3] This theme, derived from the deepest theological foundations, is the determinative rhythm of the life of the church.

John Calvin noted that the story of the church is the story of many resurrections. Such a concept should dominate our thinking about the renewal of the church today. Rather than death, we should be talking about resurrection—new life!

The church as the body of Christ is called to suffer the same fate as the physical body of its Lord. This means that the hope of Christians is not for success judged by worldly standards, but for the miracle of divine grace whereby God raises from the dead and creates out of nothing. True, individual Christians are needed for heroic efforts. But the renewal of life in the church is possible because it is the will of God, not because of heroic efforts on the part of human beings.

It dare not be the sole aim of the church to increase its prestige or its influence in the world. It must be the aim of the church to be obedient to God. God may increase the size of the church, or he may decrease it. Let us remember that no matter who plants, waters, cultivates, or gathers, it is God who gives the increase, whatever increase there may be.

## What the Churches Can Do

Every city of size has downtown and suburban churches. The problems of each have been much written about. There is a third group of churches in a city that are neither downtown nor suburban. Perhaps these were once fast-growing suburban areas, but now they have stabilized and not many new people move in. It is easy for such a church to reach a plateau and become static. Even the members grow restless because there is so little numerical growth.

In one major city, the pastor and associate pastor of six such churches gathered in regular discussions to talk over their mutual areas of concern. In this group were two Roman Catholic churches, one Methodist, one Presbyterian, one Disciples of Christ, and one Baptist. Oddly enough, the group originated, not in the thinking of the pastors, but with associate pastors and ministers of education who felt that they faced the same kind of problems and were curious to see how the others dealt with similar matters. Then the pastors were asked to join these monthly sessions.

In the beginning, the discussions were more or less of the "getting to know you" variety. Each denomination explained its denominational polity, told the procedures, how various agencies functioned, and so on. Each expressed amazement at the loosely knit structure of the Baptist and the Disciples. "How do you ever get anything done?" they asked.

Later talks centered around neighborhood peculiarities, one of which was the close intermingling of white and Negro housing. Consideration was given to the type of church program needed to minister to a membership, some of whose members drove fifteen miles to church. (This was totally new to the Roman Catholics, with their circumscribed parish lines.) Many varieties of activities for youth and adults have been talked about. And, of course, the usual topics of budgets, finance campaigns, and membership turnover got a share of attention.

Then, the broader issues of the total ecumenical movement—both Protestant and Roman Catholic—came in for much talk. This particular group of leaders expressed no interest in union, but did see much reason for unity. The occasion offered a way to explain the stated reasons for lack of Southern Baptist participation in the broader ecumenical movement, although this group is in itself a grass-roots ecumenicalism. Of course, there have been the usual jokes, jibes, and banter between the denominations; a good sense of humor is the best solvent for the grit of irritation.

What these six churches can and will accomplish, either separately or cooperatively within the area of the city where they minister, is not yet known. However, this is a beginning. The varied threads of thought, concern, and activity will produce a recognizable pattern sometime in the tomorrow. At least, each has learned the depth of concern and vitality of the other, and a healthy respect and mutual regard has developed as this group seeks ways of implementing the teachings of Christ.

This same procedure could be shared in smaller cities and towns, and even in rural areas, if we could eliminate the competitive fraternity-like rush for members and instead, think of an overall Christian witness to the community as a whole.

Size has never been the biblical equating of God's blessing. Divine approval is qualitative, not quantitative. In any case, the church must live by the evangelical law that he who would save his life must lose it, and he who loses his life for Christ's sake will find it. The church, as well as the individual Christian, must expect to find renewed life only when it learns to give itself for the world, even as Christ did.

Now, let me make a few observations before we decide about ourselves and our place as church people in this doctrine of the remnant.

For one thing, there is never any improvement without change. If we Christians are to redeem the world, we cannot be like the world. We must come apart and be different. We must be *in* the world but not *of* the world. Calling men to a better way is the inescapable business of this "saving remnant" called the church.

Second, those who advocate any specific change are always in a minority. So what? The hope of the world lies in its creative minorities. A sentence from one of Winston Churchill's wartime speeches points this out: "Never have so many owed so much to so few." Change itself does not always spell trouble, but *specific* change does!

In the next place, there is no significant minority which does not suffer. Often the suffering is nothing more than the discomfort of opposition. At other times it is actual deprivation or persecution. Sometimes it is imprisonment, and occasionally, death. Have you or I ever felt any pressure, any discomfort because of our Christian commitment? If not, we have not pushed far enough away from the total group to be known as a part of a creative minority.

There is no deep fellowship with God unless we do move adventurously forward, accepting whatever suffering may come. Without complete commitment to God's will, our lives are not fully open to accept God's promises of power. Pentecostal power comes when there is a Pentecostal task and when Christians respond with Pentecostal fervor. During the tribulations that accompany a forthright stand, many a person has found the richness of a fellowship with God which in easier days he never suspected was possible.

### Notes

1. Dietrich Bonhoeffer, *Life Together* (New York: Harper & Row, 1954), pp. 17–18.

2. Kwame Nkrumah, quoted in the *Watchman-Examiner*, February 2, 1958, p. 113.

3. Cf. John E. Cantelon, *A Protestant Approach to the Campus Ministry* (Philadelphia: The Westminster Press, 1964), pp. 109–10. Copyright 1964 W. L. Jenkins. Used by permission.

# 7

## Be Proud of the Church

### Romans 15:17,19

Pride is one of the favorite whipping boys of psychologists and preachers. Pride has taken a terrible beating. I have taken my own turn at giving pride a few lashes—someone else's pride, that is. The sum total of evils with which pride has been charged is appalling. The insights of biblical scholars, theologians, psychologists, and psychiatrists have shown pride to be not a minor blemish on our character but a major blot in individual life and on social history. Self-righteousness, self-assertion, and self-satisfaction have been forms of the pride which goes be-

fore the fall of man into grievous sin. Pride builds a strong
wall against a person's entrance into the Christian experience, for the gates into the Christian experience are
repentance and humility. And pride cannot stoop low
enough to get in.

But we have become afraid to point out the virtues in
an honest pride, the self-satisfaction in a job well done.
Along with the spiritual gain that might come in rec-
ognizing pride for what it is has come a great loss. Perhaps we need another word to express the deep and
genuine joy one has in participating in something great.
Paul exults in this kind of emotion. Several times in his
epistles Paul apologizes for what he calls "boasting," but
with him it is not mere boasting; it is honest, legitimate
pride.

It is legitimate pride in a great and noble heritage which
caused him to call attention to that fact that he was of the
people of Israel, of the tribe of Benjamin, a Hebrew born
of Hebrews, of the city of Tarsus, a citizen of Rome. There
is also a legitimate pride in his connection with the gospel,
causing him to say:

"I am not ashamed of the gospel," or, as Moffatt trans-
lates it in a more positive manner,

"I am proud of the gospel; it is God's saving power!"

In our own lives it should be that we are too proud to
stoop to corruption or bribes; lie, steal, cheat, or defraud;
be mean to or berate another person; sacrifice a principle
or a conviction for expedience or reward; risk the virtue
of a clean and pure life for the satisfying whim of a moment; be sub-Christian in falling short of the glory of God
in any way!

### Proud of the Church?

Now, let us take a look at the question Paul asked the Corinthians: "Are you still proud of your church?" (1 Cor. 5:2, Phillips*). I confess that I do have a legitimate, honest pride in the church. Don't get me wrong. The church is not perfect; far from that! My heart cries out at the failures—its inconsistencies, complacency, and evidences of pettiness. There is an ache because loyalty and support are not stronger. Pain comes because we seem to be more interested in public opinion polls than we are in prophetic voices. Nevertheless, with all of its faults, I love the church and its people.

"Are you still proud of your church?" Paul's question is directed at the people of Corinth, who were condoning gross immorality. He implies that there was once cause for pride; but what about now? There are tears mixed with anger in this query. How can anyone be proud of a church which has yielded to the moral stain of its environment? The church is not to take on the characteristics of the community. The church is to change the community into the likeness of Christ.

The reproach is all the stronger when we remember how much Paul loved the church. It is because he loves it so dearly and deeply that he feels keenly the shame brought upon it. Is this not true in our own experience? The more we love, the more we are hurt when the object of our love breaks down. Paul's ideal of the church is expressed in this picture of what the church ought to be:

* From *The New Testament in Modern English*, © J. B. Phillips, 1958. Used with permission of the Macmillan Company.

Christ loved the church and gave himself up for her, that he might sanctify her, having cleansed her by the washing of water with the word, that the church might be presented before him in splendor, without spot or wrinkle or any such thing, that she might be holy and without blemish (Eph. 5:25–27, RSV).

Dorothy Sayers once made a list of the modern "seven deadly sins" which may afflict a church. Some of her listings represent a shameful compromise with a non-Christian culture. Others are a failure to show the love of Christ to people. Here is her list: respectability, childishness, mental timidity, dulness, sentimentality, censoriousness, and depression of spirit.

All of these add up to an illegitimate pride which causes us to say, "We've got it made. We're pretty good. Look us over." Can we be proud of such an attitude? It is truly a deadly sin. It kills. It kills the very spirit which is the life of the church. The spirit of the church should be that which Jesus described in the parable of the lost sheep— the unsatisfied heart of the shepherd. What a name for a church—*the church of the unsatisfied shepherd!*

There is a well-known church whose Indian name means, "The End of the Road." In an ultra-affluent suburb, this is translated as "We have arrived. We've got it made!" Most of us have made the church a congregation of satisfied sheep.

Can we be proud of our restrictions? We teach our children to sing:

> Jesus loves the little children,
> All the children of the world;
> Red and yellow, black and white,

They are precious in his sight;
Jesus loves the little children of the world.

Then we fail to let those same little children come into
the church where they can learn of this Jesus whom we
say loves them. We adults sing:

> In Christ there is no East or West,
> In Him no South or North,
> But one great fellowship of love
> Throughout the whole wide earth.[1]

But do we practice what we sing? Not when we spend
hours of debate on whether or not the Negro will be al-
lowed to worship. Not when we say he cannot worship.
And not when we exclude anyone of color from membership solely on that basis. The church is not meant to
exclude. Christ excluded no one. A person may exclude
himself, but the church dare not exclude anyone who
acknowledges Christ as Lord.

Shakespeare used an interesting figure of speech about
the church in *Romeo and Juliet*. Mercutio, Romeo's friend,
is wounded in a street fight. When asked about his wound,
he says: " 'Tis not so deep as a well, nor so wide as a
church door; but 'tis enough, 'twill serve." So! A church
door was one of the widest things Shakespeare could
think of. And why not? Do we not sing, "There's a wideness in God's mercy/Like the wideness of the sea"? But
do we demonstrate that wideness? Ay, there's the rub!

### Self-Study Programs

Having listened to Paul's question, now listen to his
claim: "I have reason to be proud of my work for God."

Paul rejoiced in the right kind of pride, that is, "in Jesus Christ." This is a ministry beautifully described by Henry Sloane Coffin, who said the work of a Christian is "to take the hands of men and women and put them into the hand of God." Are we doing that, you and I? Is our church, yours and mine?

The words of an actor in describing the skill of a dramatic producer, describe unintentionally the high calling of Christian service: "his ability to make actors and actresses rise above their normal talent, and form, . . . what it would be over simple to call . . . a living pattern."

This is a part of the work of a Christian and of a church: to bring the enabling spirit of Christ into a person's life, to place his hand in the hand of God, so that he will rise above his natural level of talent, and become a part of a living pattern, a pattern which reproduces Christlike character.

What about us? Have we done that, you and I? Yes, despite our failures, there are evidences that we have done that, that we are doing something to help people produce lives in the pattern of a living faith.

Dare we look at our work for God as if we were strangers called in to make an objective appraisal, seeing our work for the first time? How willing are we to look? How honest would we be?

Business, industry, and colleges have many "self studies." Churches are beginning to do this, too. The appointment of a long-range planning committee is the first step. Pilot projects have been guided by the Church Administration Department of the Baptist Sunday School Board (cf. *A Church Organized and Functioning*, by W. L.

Howse and W. O. Thomason). Perhaps some needed guidelines for all churches will come of these projects.

One of the "pilot project" churches prefaced its third report to the church with these words:

This report is based on our present knowledge and vision of the kind of church we must become by 1974, in order to meet changing community requirements and carry out our functions as a church.[2]

After listing some tentative long-range goals, they made specific recommendations for congregational action. Then they spelled out those actions by allotting a certain amount of time for each: 1964–65; 1966–69; 1970–74. This was done in six areas: worshiping, proclaiming, educating, ministering, administrative services, and program services.

Another church, acting on its own prior to these pilot projects and not having any guidelines, set up a five-point, five-year program of advance. Their self-study included the areas of evangelism, education, worship, missions, and stewardship. A staff member and a deacon were members of each of these five committees, along with other church members. Nearly a year was taken for the study. Each committee was asked to submit a one-page summary of its total findings as well as a written report of its work and suggestions. Mimeographed copies were presented to all the deacons. Sections were presented on Wednesday nights. Particular details were handed to proper persons and committees for implementation.[3]

Many churches are asking serious questions about the meaning of church membership. Some churches have set up membership committees to interview prospective applications. Instead of voting to receive members at the time the request is made, this is delayed until some personal visitation and discussion has been done. Then a recommendation is made to the church at a regular business meeting. Many Northern churches have done this for many years, but it is relatively new in the South. Such a move has led to significant developments in making church membership more meaningful.

One church, after much prayerful talk, did not advocate a membership committee, but they did recommend that a broad study of the meaning and significance of church membership be conducted. It was first suggested that the Training Union use the Southern Baptist special training series on church membership. However, to insure broader coverage, it was decided that the Sunday School should use it.

Most denominations have more resources available than churches generally use. Often churches do not even know what is available. This is certainly true of the Southern Baptist Convention. For example, if a church wanted a stimulating week of emphasis dealing with pertinent social concerns, the Christian Life Commission would be a good place to begin. Here is an outline of a very successful week already tried in several churches.

> Monday night—"Alcohol and Narcotics"
> Tuesday night—"Salacious Literature"
> Wednesday night—"The Christian Home"
> Thursday night—"Church-State Relations"
> Friday night—"Race Relations"

The plan generally is for the same speaker to discuss each of these topics in about a forty-five minute address. Following a refreshment break, the group reassembles for detailed discussion on each subject. If these subjects do not have lively appeal, there are others equally valuable. The Christian Life Commission has excellent printed material on these and other subjects. For some of this material there is a nominal charge, but a portion is free for the asking.

It might be possible to secure one of the Commission staff members as the major speaker. If not, one might at least be available to help plan such a week for any interested church, and there are plenty of other qualified persons to speak, such as the professors of Christian ethics at our Baptist seminaries.

A variation on this method was an invitation to one of the seminary professors of church history to speak for a week on the theme, "The Baptist Heritage and Its Witness for Our Times."

This week met a definite need in the lives of many people who had been Baptists all their lives, but were woefully weak in knowledge of why they were Baptists in the first place, or continued to be.

### The Full Gospel

Were I to take a look at my own work, there are a few places and a few things about which I feel good. Maybe on a rare occasion something is even worth legitimate pride. But far too often I would have to admit that pettiness has crept in, personal peeves have blocked my vision of God, motives have not always been purely unselfish, and convictions have on occasion been soft-pedaled for fear of stirring up controversy that might jeopardize personal security or alienate some church member.

Of that I am not proud. There is too much cause for shame. There have been those times when opportunities have been missed, or bungled—not so much from wilful wrongdoing as from just not doing right, or doing the right thing for the wrong reason. Sometimes the wrong method has been used. At other times there has been simple neglect. And there have been those times when a choice to do one thing left another thing undone, and the choice proved to be unwise.

But there is a genuine sense in which you or I as individual Christians can say with Paul: "I have reason to be proud of my work for God" (Rom. 15:17, RSV). Note two things: first, the phrase "in Jesus Christ" which immediately precedes Paul's statement.

Then, read the verses following and notice this clause: "I have fully preached the gospel of Christ."

I doubt if in the largest sense Paul himself would have made such a claim. In the passage here Paul is speaking, thinking, and writing principally in "geographic" terms, "So that from Jerusalem and as far around as Illyricum I have fully preached the gospel of Christ" (v. 19).

What he means is that if one of us does his work "in Jesus Christ," speaking nothing except what Christ has done so that wherever we go, whatever we may do the gospel is fully preached and openly practiced, then we have no cause for shame.

Even so, who among us would make such a claim as Paul makes? Only one who has failed to plumb the depths

or measure the range of the gospel would so dare. Or, one
who has failed to see the ordeals and the aching needs of
today's world. Or, one who has little concern or compassion for people—all kinds, shapes, and colors of people. In
other words, only the satisfied shepherd or the satisfied
sheep can be proud.

We can preach the gospel geographically. But it is the
word "fully" which disturbs me. It bows us to our knees.
It is an adverb too high for us. We cannot attain unto it.
At this word "fully" we all fall short.

It is so much easier to preach "partly" the gospel, leav-
ing out the parts that deal with the dangerous, contro-
versial areas of our life and world. So we can spend our
time catering to our prejudices or accepting the moral
and spiritual limitations of a group.

The Master said, "Go into all the world and preach the
gospel." Can you imagine Jesus going through the streets
of our city—the streets not usually included in the guided
tours we provide for visitors, or even a few of those we
discreetly show—seeing the need, the neglect, the sordid
conditions, and asking: "Has my gospel been fully
preached here?"

Peter's sermon at Pentecost is usually described as the
first Christian sermon. Peter's hearers on that occasion
did not yawn and go sleepily on their way. They were
"cut to the heart!" A fully preached gospel must be one
that cuts. Of course, it binds up wounds and it heals broken hearts, *but it also cuts!* And it is not true that men
respond to the intensity with which a cause is presented.
Men want a call to action, not a soothing lullaby. Men
want drums, not soft Melachrino Strings. And in a fully

preached gospel there can always be heard the roll of drums beating a charge, not a retreat.

Let me conclude by turning to the basic reason why Paul could introduce himself to the Roman Christians as one who had a right to be proud of the work he had done in preaching the gospel. We find it in Romans 1:16: "I am not ashamed of the gospel of Christ: for it is the power of God unto salvation to every one that believeth." The Moffatt translation has a more accurate meaning: "I am proud of the gospel; it is God's saving power for everyone who has faith."

If there is any cause for shame, it is in us; not in the gospel, for the gospel is God's saving power. And anyone who has faith will know and experience that power.

There are those not identified with the Christian faith or with the church. To you we believing Christians apologize for our failures toward Christ and the gospel. Do not let one of us stand in your way. We do have the treasure, but it is in earthen vessels. Do not let the vessel lessen the value of the treasure or keep you from being another container of it.

### Notes

1. Used by permission of the American Tract Society.

2. From a mimeographed report of the First Baptist Church, Monroe, Louisiana, April 29, 1964.

3. A similar program for the rural church is sponsored by the Southern Baptist Home Mission Board. Details may be secured by writing.

# 8

## A Church and Its Affirmations

### Philippians 3:1–16;4:4–7

To be the pastor of a church is a delightful, charming, exciting, challenging, demanding task. At times it can be frustrating, baffling, and perturbing. One of the bafflements is the complacent indifference that meets many efforts to "do something." Too often a church is content to *look*, and not make the effort to do something challenging and demanding.

Most churches pride themselves on being different, on saying, "Ours is a peculiar church, you know." There are distinctive differences, even among Baptist churches. But how often do we sit down to analyze those differences and then go out and share those valid differences with others?

There are many cries being raised these days about a "class church." I would certainly agree that no church ought to become exclusively class-conscious in denying its worship or membership to anyone—*anyone*—who feels that his spiritual needs can be best met by a particular church. However, some people exclude themselves because they do not feel comfortable in a particular group of people. There should never be a church that exclusively classifies itself; but if people classify and exclude themselves, that is another matter.

A church ought to offer reverence, beauty, and dignity in its worship, the highest quality of what is best in sacred music, a broad spirit of missionary-evangelistic concern, deep social compassion, a relevant pulpit ministry that is "geared to the times but anchored to the rock," and a warmhearted fellowship. The church should then take all that and match it with the concern and commitment of sharing, a wholehearted participation, a devotion that believes in what it is doing, and a sense of dependable responsibility. No one could foresee the future of such a church as that!

I have never been one to play upon a person's sense of guilt in order to get him to do something in and for the church. A Christian should be motivated by the love of God, Christ, and the church to give of his best in service. But, somehow, the sense of guilt and fear seems to motivate people more than do love and concern.

Most people love the church, especially the church to which they belong, with all their hearts. But for the life of me, I find it hard to grasp the indifference that freedom within the church has produced. Freedom—*in anything*—must have an accompanying sense of responsibility. Among many church people, seemingly, there is a freedom from old restraints, legalisms, and demands rather than a responsibility toward sharing, developing, and maturing in Christian faith. We may decry those whom we call fundamentalists or hyperactivists, but unless we can match them in a zeal for what we consider a better way, we have lost more than we have gained.

Through the centuries Christians have met to draw up statements or creeds that affirm their faith in Jesus Christ. Usually, these creeds were hammered out on anvils of current controversy. The best known examples are The Apostles' Creed and the Nicene Creed. While we Baptists are not a creedal people, we have also found it necessary at times to draw up covenants of faith or statements of faith. The best known of the older efforts are The Philadelphia Confession of Faith and The New Hampshire Confession of Faith. Each of these shows a bit of bias toward a specific understanding of Baptist beliefs. Our most recent examples are the statement of faith adopted by the Southern Baptist Convention meeting in Kansas City in 1963, and *Baptist Ideals*, a statement used for the Third Baptist Jubilee Celebration in Atlantic City, New Jersey, in 1964.

These statements, or affirmations, are supposed to be a kind of common meeting ground upon which the various segments of Baptists can unite and agree. They are not considered as binding, and certainly are not to be used as tests of fellowship or standards of orthodoxy. We Baptists pride ourselves in our "fellowship of difference" despite occasional efforts on the part of some to make their fellow

Baptists conform to their particular views. In all differences, there must be intellectual, moral, and spiritual integrity. Therefore, let me submit five affirmations which I consider vital for a church.

The first would be *biblical affirmation*—a common belief among us that our faith is a revealed faith and the source of that revelation is the Bible.

That may sound strange coming from a Baptist, for we Baptists have always considered the Bible to be our sole guide and authority in spiritual matters. We have considered ourselves to be "a people of the Book," (although some among us have wanted to choose those parts of the Book we would be a people of). We have never fully agreed on what specifically constitutes the inspiration and authority of the Bible, but we have agreed that it stands as our basic guide. We say, "The Bible as the inspired revelation of God's will and way, made full and complete in the life and teachings of Christ, is our authoritative rule of faith and practice." [1]

Perhaps we have assumed that because we say this, we automatically observe it. But such is not the case. Even in our Sunday Schools, supposed to be our Bible teaching agency, we have been lax. Whatever the teaching method, we must not neglect the actual content of the Bible. Necessary as it is to make biblical application to current situations, we need to know the actual content before we can make proper applications. We need to know much about the Bible: its origins, how we got it, its overall teachings, and what those teachings mean. This calls for a careful combination of content and application.

Next, there needs to be *doctrinal affirmation*. Why are

we Baptists, anyway? What makes us different from any other Christians, especially other Protestant Christians? If we Baptists do not have some doctrinal affirmations, some distinctives, then is there any real reason for us to exist as a denomination? If we do have such distinctive affirmations, then we need to know what they are.

As for me, I am a Baptist by personal choice and conviction, but I am not a Baptist-and-a-half! I do believe we have some distinctives worth preserving. In some cases the lines are not as sharply drawn nor as deeply etched as they were a few hundred years ago, or even fifty years ago. Whether our ideas are rubbing off on others, or theirs on us, is hard to say. It is preferable to believe that ours are having influence on others, especially in such an area as religious freedom. It bothers me that, on the one hand, some Baptists do not see any valid distinctions about the denomination, while on the other hand some Baptists try to make us far more than we actually are with their unbroken line of apostolic succession as one example which is neither scripturally nor historically accurate.

Surely we ought to affirm the basic Christian doctrines we share with all Christians, and we must maintain our Baptist expression of such doctrines.

These, along with such other principles as religious liberty, an open-minded searching of the Scriptures, and the commission to evangelize the world in the name of Christ, are important to us.

Third, we need *evangelical affirmation.* The source of our strength and power through the centuries has been our deep concern that the gospel be preached to all the world. The need of people is as great and the gospel we proclaim is as valid as ever. I, for one, am glad to see us break away from some of our old methods of evangelism where we use all sorts of tricks, gimmicks, and emotional persuasions to manipulate people. Let us rejoice in every new approach that brings us into the arenas of life where people live. But in moving out into the world let us not take on the coloration of conformity to the world.

Vice-president Albert Bailey told a recent meeting of the British Methodist Conference that for them it was "evangelize or perish." He said that they need not look to union with the Church of England to solve their problems. These days, in which Christianity is taking a beating on every hand, do also see a lot of Christians trying to solve their problems by merger or by moving to new areas rather than by employing evangelical witness where they are. Merging or moving away may bring some statistical satisfaction, but that is about all.

Evangelism made us Baptists what we are. The methods of our unsophisticated fathers met the needs of the rural culture of their day. But Southern Baptists are no longer rural. It is true that most of our churches are in rural areas, but 60 percent of our people live in urban areas and have church membership in city churches. Today we must meet the sophistication of the scientific mind, the high-rise apartment environment, the suburban culture, and the urban enlightenment.

On every side of us are people who need an encounter that makes Christ real to them. The problem of personal sin affects us all, in some way or other. Just how we are to bring the good news to bear, to get the message of Christ across in our day, I do not know; but we must try. We can invite in a neighbor, we can have lunch with a business associate, we can tell what the Christian faith means to us. We can at least let our children know that the church and Christian faith are important to us. Evangelism is not so much method as it is message, and our message is the sufficiency of Jesus Christ to meet the needs of life.

### Hand in Hand

The fourth affirmation would be *relevance*. This is a terribly overworked word, and not as easy to define as it is to say. I guess it literally means to face real issues and everyday problems: *today's* issues and problems, that is. We dare not isolate ourselves in some ivory tower of ecclesiastical "busyness" while the issues and problems of today get solved outside the Christian context. We must concern ourselves with poverty, substandard housing, rising crime statistics, racial involvements, war, and the like.

There are many Christian groups with a deep social concern and an almost total lack of evangelism that fail to witness to the saving grace of Christ. There are also Christians who rejoice loudly over the success of their evangelistic efforts, but whose voices are mere whispers on the subject of social justice.

Somehow, we need to plant ourselves firmly between the two, giving a vital, valid witness to both these dimensions of the Christian faith. Only people transformed by the grace of God can truly transform society. But transformed people are called upon to live, act, speak, and do according to the gospel imperative in whatever situation they may find themselves.

Finally, I would propose *ecumenical affirmation*. This is

not the most popular of the five. God has other children whom he loves and for whom Christ died who are not Southern Baptists. That may come as a surprise to some. In fact, there are far more of them than there are of us. Now, to be sure, we ought to reaffirm our own heritage, our convictions, our biblical rootage, and our denominational affirmations. But we should not be afraid to join hands and hearts with those other disciples of Christ. We do have some common objectives in carrying out the commission of Christ. There is no future for us in isolationism. And I really question if there is any future in organic union or merger. But there is a great future for brethren who dwell and work together in unity.

There are many things about the World Council and the National Council of Churches that I do not like. But I would like to see us working within those frameworks and trying to bring about change from the inside. The newly formed Louisiana Council of Churches leaves some things to be desired, but I would like to see us a part of that Council and try to make it more desirable. The Greater New Orleans Federation of Churches and the United Council of Church Women have weaknesses, but I am glad that we have been a part of them since their foundation. We were the first Baptist church in the city to join the Federation, and we are the only Baptist church with continuous membership.

Says one Baptist historian:

A denomination needs to prove its right to continue to exist, not by looking backwards, but by indicating its capacity to contribute significantly and relevantly to the life of the church in the modern age. If the mission of the church is to reduce all human boundaries and barriers, and if the church is really the whole people of God, then we as Baptists must be prepared to do three things:

1. To acknowledge that God has worked through each denomination, including our own, in spite of the incompleteness of each.

2. To recognize that no denomination, including our own, has laid hold of the fulness of God's provision for his church.

3. To seek together a fuller life of faith and order in the consciousness that the unity of the church is the fruit of a loyalty to Jesus Christ which transcends all bounds and surmounts all human barriers.[3]

Great winds of change are blowing across the churches of the world these days, and the ecumenical spirit of the World Council of Churches and the Roman Catholic Vatican Council II are largely responsible. Many are saying it is the rushing, mighty wind of God called the Holy Spirit. And it may well be; I do not know. But I do know that there is a new vitality, awareness, and concern, and I do not want to be left out or passed by. None of us dare ignore the fast-running ecumenical tide. On the other hand, we must not let ourselves be swept into an open sea of some organic superchurch. I feel that we can have a fuller expression of ecumenicity and more cooperation without any loss of our distinctives and with no diminishing of our convictions.

Now, where do we begin implementing these affirmations? Naturally, it must start with the pastor, but all members of a church need to be a part of it as well. Therefore, there is a call, not just to affirmations, but to commitment and work! This is no time for draftees; we need volunteers, those who are convinced. It is a time for vacationers from responsibility to come back and settle down. Perhaps some vacations need to be postponed for awhile. We cannot afford the luxury of lackadaisical attitude and effort. We need dependability and stability. This is a time for advance. Thoreau once said: "If a man does not keep pace with his companions, perhaps it is because he hears a different drummer. Let him keep step to the music he hears, however measured or far away."

It is important what music we hear and march to. I remember in a high school speech class having to memorize a poem about a drummer boy during battle time (this was in the days before walkie-talkies when troops were signaled by certain beats of the drum). The battle was not going very well; so the captain went to the drummer and said: "Beat a retreat!" Came the reply, "Sir, I do not know how to beat a retreat. But I can beat a charge; O, I can beat a charge!"

*And he did!*

## Notes

1. *Baptist Ideals.* Pamphlet prepared by the Committee on Baptist Ideals, and published by the Sunday School Board of the Southern Baptist Convention, Nashville, Tennessee, 1963, p. 7.

2. *Ibid.,* pp. 11, 15, 18.

3. Quoted from Robert Torbet's address to the American Baptist Convention of 1966, *The Watchman-Examiner* (June, 1966).

# 9

## What's Right with the Church?*

### Isaiah 51:1–6; Matthew 21:42

A woman writing in a national magazine a few years ago remarked that in her early career, she turned from the church because it seemed to her to have too little contact with either the first century or the twentieth to be significant. She said: "Surely, we have a right to expect that the church shall be in contact with reality somewhere." In other words, she was saying that today's church is both unbiblical and irrelevant.

The use of *either/or* may suggest that it is possible for the church to have contact with either the first century or

* I am indebted to a rabbi friend for the germinal ideas in this chapter.

118

the twentieth without having contact with both. Such is not the case. Biblical authenticity and modern relevance should be two sides of the same coin. However, judging from much evidence, the criticism has validity. There are indications that in many of today's churches there is neither biblical nor social relevance. In some churches there may be one or the other. And perhaps in a few, there may be both.

Our generation has gone about the task of demolishing the past with a will, but there is little to show for our efforts except wreckage and desolation. The shattered and discredited traditions have so far yielded little but chaos and confusion. Revolt seems to be the characteristic mood of our day, but it is too often revolt without the accompanying responsibility of creating something better than that against which we revolt. We may not like what we have, but have we the right to destroy it unless we can replace it with something better?

Whatever else the efforts of our contemporary artists may reveal to the expert critics, they show two things to the casual observer: First, a vigorous rejection of both the forms and the concepts of the past; and second, a terrifying, but accurate reflection of the disarrangement of our modern life—humanly, morally, emotionally, and spiritually.

Many of the art forms of our time are on the one hand a daring effort at experimentation. But on the other hand they are an appalling manifestation of the broken fragments of a Humpty-Dumpty age that is incapable of putting itself together into a recognizable unity of will, spirit, or purpose. From the shambles of our torn society come the agonized voices of an age that is bereft of hope, has abandoned trust in the past, and feels nothing but futility for the future.

Yet, from out of the shattering alienation of the soul of modern man, a voice cries out from the remote past: "Look to the rock from which you were hewn." This is a call to look for truth not only, as we must, in the dark crevices of the present, but to peer into the past as well. So the cry continues: "Listen to me, my people, for a law will go forth from me . . . My deliverance draws near . . . My salvation has gone forth."

*Look to the rock!* The ancient rock of a half-forgotten, dimly remembered past offers us eternal truth. The stone which the builders rejected offers the chief cornerstone for today's personal life as well as that of mankind. Like Gibraltar the church stands, built upon a rock. The forces of revolt, disregard, and discord beat upon that rock, but they cannot prevail against the church. Hurricane winds beat upon it and tides sweep over it, but the church stands —and will continue to stand.

Whatever we cling to in our storm-tossed lives must be seized by *us*. Even if some buoy has been hurled out from the God of eternity, we must grasp it and make it our own.

There must be personal faith on our part before there can be a collective faith.

I submit that there are some fragments of the eternal rock which are basic to Christian faith and thus to the church. We must look back to them and grasp them if we are ever to be able to look forward. The fundamental rightness of the church is that it is built upon such a rock.

### Historic Truth

First, there is the rock of *historic truth*.

It has been my privilege on several occasions to walk over parts of the ancient world, where archaeological ruins remind us of "The glory that was Greece, And the grandeur that was Rome." [1] As one walks where Jesus walked in the section we call the Holy Land, he sees an area that for centuries has been crisscrossed by an endless procession of civilizations. Up the highways from Egypt came the armies and caravans of the world-subduing pharaohs. Here the Philistines established themselves and became the terror of a land upon whose history they branded their name. Syria, Assyria, Babylonia, Persia, and others are well remembered. Here Doric columns testify to the political, cultural, and religious influence exerted by Greece. Here are remnants reminding us that Rome held empires in the shadow of her deities and emperors. Here Muslims left their mosques, Crusaders left their castles, and Turks left remains that lie intermingled like the bleached bones of fallen dead in a desert battlefield.

Seeing all this, one senses an uncanny feeling of participation in this passing parade. It reminds us of the transiency of our own world. Nations must become humble and civilizations contrite, for there is no endurance in power and grandeur. Supremacy hovers for a brief moment over a favored people, then is gone. The mantle passes to some other people.

From our limited perspective, the lesson of dry bones is tragic and gloomy. Must we, too, walk that lonely road into oblivion and be remembered and measured by the relics of a few crumbled buildings and a few scraps of literature?

Those dry bones issue a call to hope for our time. That hope stems from the reminder that *God is no respecter of civilizations* any more than he is of persons. God's spirit always hovers, even if over a void. The enduring Spirit of the living God waits to breathe life upon a new day in human experience when nations and civilizations will abide side by side, rather than be buried one on top of the other.

Too often we Christians take it for granted that historic truth is significant. In reality it is an unusual belief. Most religions outside the Judeo-Christian tradition look at history as meaningless. For them, man has nothing better to do than to escape from it all, the best way he can— *if he can.*

Even the professional historians, with a few exceptions such as Arnold Toynbee, take a dim view of one who dares to draw lessons from this rise and fall of civilizations.

History, according to Christian faith, is the story of God's dealings with men. In the events of human experience there is both plan and purpose. The Bible tells the story of a particular people, the Jews, as if their story had universal significance. And it does! All people know slavery, freedom, exile, sin, and hope. And all men are offered a covenant of deliverance with God.

Paul Tillich says, "From the Christian standpoint the center of history is the appearance of Jesus as the Christ." In other words, the main clue to history's meaning is the birth, life, teachings, death, and resurrection of Jesus.

Here is revealed the nature of God and the purpose of man. The universe is not just brute force or meaningless motion. The world operates within a framework of moral law as well as within natural law. It is in Jesus Christ that God reveals himself completely. Jesus Christ is the assurance that human history has meaning.

It is to the church that the task of keeping alive this truth has been committed. And it is to this rock of historic truth that we must anchor ourselves when it appears that everything nailed down is coming loose.

### Divine Truth

The second foundation upon which the church is built is the *rock of divine truth.*

After the second Russian cosmonaut made his orbits around the earth, Nikita Khrushchev delivered a theological verdict, declaring that his cosmonaut had passed through the heavens again and again and had come upon no evidence of angels, or any celestial creatures, or even of God. In *Honest to God* Bishop J. A. T. Robinson chides us for referring to God as *up* there or *out* there. God cannot be placed or located.

In the late eighteenth century there was a pietistic movement among the Jews of Eastern Europe called the Chasidim. This movement saved a vast portion of Jewry from despair and disintegration. One of the leaders of that movement was Rabbi Zev Wolf, who wrote a one-volume commentary on the Bible. In it, he renders Psalm 139:8 ("If I mount up to heaven, thou art there") this way: "Were I to mount up to the heavens, thou wouldst be there, *beyond.*"

In this penetrating insight Rabbi Wolf expressed truth without which religious faith becomes impotent: that however far we penetrate beyond the frontiers of time or space, *God is there, beyond!* The Creator of the universe who proclaims, "Let there be!" the Judge who commands, "Thou shalt not!" the Redeemer who calls, "Whosoever will may come," the Saviour who assures, "Whoever comes will not be turned away," *is there!*

We Christians believe that our faith is divine truth. We boldly (sometimes) proclaim its universal inclusiveness to all who will believe in Christ as Saviour and follow him as Lord. However, we often fail to point out its narrow exclusivism. When Jesus says, "I and the Father are one . . . no one comes to the Father except by me" (John 10:30, RSV, 14:6, NEB), he is placing severe restrictions. So, at the same time, Christianity is broadly inclusive and narrowly restrictive. Presenting these claims to people of other faiths is a delicate matter. It must be done with sincerity and honest recognition of differences. An approach does not always bring immediate results. But, are we responsible for results or for witnessing? Two episodes are illustrative.

More than 150 Roman Catholics in Beaufort, South Carolina, met with Southern Baptists for a joint worship service in which Baptist doctrines were expounded.

This unique service was held at the invitation of the deacons of the Baptist Church of Beaufort. Almost all of the local Catholic church members attended, according to George A. Jones, the Baptist pastor.

Immediately following the service, Ronald P. Anderson, pastor of St. Peter's Catholic Church, said:

We have felt the presence of the Holy Spirit here tonight. We accepted the most gracious invitation of our Baptist friends to join them in their worship service that we might observe their form of worship, that we might share together the Word of God, and that we might unite our prayers that, as God wills, and in the way He wills, there might be one truly Christian family." [2]

I recently invited the Jewish rabbi of the synagogue nearest our church to preach for an evening service of worship. A graduate of a Methodist college, Rabbi Julian Feibleman had spoken in many Christian churches, but had never been asked to preach. It was a most worshipful occasion. A large number of the synagogue members attended. Hymns were chosen that would not embarrass the Jewish visitors, but which would proclaim faith in God. Following the rabbi's sermon, I explained the Baptist custom of giving a public invitation for people to make a decision regarding faith in God, especially in Jesus Christ. During the singing of the invitation hymn, two people asked for membership in this Baptist church.

A few weeks later, I was extended an invitation to be the first Christian minister to preach for a regular Sabbath service of worship in New Orleans' Temple Sinai. In the sermon, I took three sentences at the close of the sermon as a positive statement of Christian faith. While it cannot be called "Jewish evangelism," at least a rapport was established that did not exist before.

### Moral Truth

The third foundation of the church is the *rock of moral truth*.

Standing before Michelangelo's *Moses* in St. Peter-in-Chains Church in Rome is an unforgettable experience of awed reverence. Never yet in repeated visits have I had my fill of looking, wondering, and praying.

More awesome than the genius of Michelangelo who chiseled out this stone image of the prophet of God with the brooding eyes, commanding mouth, poised as if ready to leap out from the stone at God's behest, is the slowly penetrating awareness that the stone tablets in his hands are intact!

This is the man who had been with God on Mt. Sinai, who had received the Law, who had seen the people in the depravity of sin, who had then smashed the tablets to bits. This is the man who then went back, hammered out the Law anew, and brought it back to the people as the Law of God.

There is a tradition among the Jews that as the children of Israel marched through the wilderness, the Ark of the Covenant which they carried contained the fragments of the original set as well as the second set of tablets. What does this symbolize? What does Moses' holding the tablets intact mean?

It means that however often man succumbs, God does not let him surrender. However dissolute he may become, however sophisticated he may consider himself, man still remains under God's mandate. Even when it is shattered, the Law of God is not repealed, and it is rewritten word for word for each new generation: "I am the Lord thy God!"

Moral law is from God and is not subject to any popular referendum. It is important for us to know that our age, as have all other ages, will be judged by that Law. It is necessary for us to realize that beyond all other factors making for the mad savagery of our world lies the fact of man's rebelling against God and his word of moral law.

### Spiritual Truth

There is one other foundation of the church we should consider: the *rock of spiritual truth.*

The Scriptures say: "Look to the rock from which you were hewn . . . a law will go forth from me . . . my deliverance draws near . . . my salvation has gone forth." Judaism kept alive the teaching that a messiah would bring this deliverance and salvation. Christian faith proclaims that in Jesus of Nazareth the salvation of God has come: "Thou shalt call his name Jesus, for he shall save his people from their sins" (Matt. 1:21).

There is the smell of death in the air of the world. That smell comes from the gas chambers of Auschwitz, from the radioactive rubble of Hiroshima, from the napalm bombings in Viet Nam, as well as from the foul winds of war, riot, and commotion all over the world. This smell comes because men, in trying to banish God and feeling free of all restraint, have lunged against each other in brutality.

But God's mandate stands fast, and therein is the freshener of the world's air. God's covenant with man is not annulled, and in this rests our hope. The day will come when we will go reeling in guilt in search of forgiveness and will rediscover in the oft-shattered but never annihilated tablets of God's Word, held firmly in the hands of his servants, the way of redemption.

Let me repeat an earlier paragraph: "Whatever we cling to in our storm-tossed lives must be seized by us. Even if it has been hurled out from the God of eternity, we must grasp it and make it our own."

We may look to the rock, we may recognize that Jesus Christ is the rejected stone upon which we must build, "for no other foundation can any one lay than that which is laid, which is Jesus Christ" (1 Cor. 3:11, RSV).

But unless we personally encounter Christ and make him the great rock foundation of life, he is meaningless. God's salvation *has* gone forth in Jesus Christ. There is historic truth, divine truth, moral truth, spiritual truth here to guide us. However, all this has only begun our salvation. It has not achieved it. The action of God in salvation is completed only when each of us acknowledges Christ as Saviour—only when we look to that rock, and anchor ourselves to it.

God's salvation in Jesus Christ as mere historical fact is not redemption in itself. It becomes our salvation only when in the personal decision of repentant faith we accept Christ as Saviour and the Law of God is laid intact in our hands as a sacred trust.

"Look to the rock from which you were hewn."

"Listen to me, my people, my salvation has gone forth."

"By grace are you saved through faith."

"As many as received him, to them gave he power to become the sons of God."

*Notes*

1. Edgar Allan Poe, "To Helen," stanza 2.

2. Ronald P. Anderson, quoted in the *Baptist Standard,* February 23, 1966, p. 15.